OCCASIONAL PAPER 92

Stabilization and Structural Reform in the Czech and Slovak Federal Republic: First Stage

Bijan B. Aghevli, Eduardo Borensztein,
and Tessa van der Willigen

INTERNATIONAL MONETARY FUND
Washington DC
March 1992

Library of Congress Cataloging-in-Publication Data

Aghevli, Bijan B.
Stabilization and structural reform in the Czech and Slovak Federal Republic: First stage / Bijan B. Aghevli, Eduardo Borensztein, and Tessa van der Willigen.
p. cm. — (Occasional Paper ; 92)
Includes bibliographical references.
ISBN 1-55775-226-5
1. Czechoslovakia—Economic policy—1989– 2. Economic stabilization—Czechoslovakia. I. Borensztein, Eduardo. II. Van der Willigen, Tessa. III. Title. IV. Series: Occasional paper (International Monetary Fund) ; no. 92.
HC270.282.A34 1992
339.5'09437—dc20 92-7788
CIP

Price: US$15.00
(US$12.00 to full-time faculty members and
students at universities and colleges)

Please send orders to:
International Monetary Fund, Publication Services
700 19th Street, N.W., Washington, D.C. 20431, U.S.A.
Tel.: (202) 623-7430 Telefax: (202) 623-7201

Contents

Charts

Statistical Appendix

Preface

On January 1, 1991, the Czech and Slovak Federal Republic launched a comprehensive reform program designed to establish a market economy. The program has been successful in achieving price stability and a viable external position through restrictive financial policies, but there has been a sharp decline in output. The eventual output recovery is predicated on completing structural market reforms, such as developing financial markets and safeguarding their stability, privatizing large enterprises, minimizing government interference with economic signals, and imposing the "hard" budget constraint.

The information discussed in this paper was collected during staff visits to Czechoslovakia during 1990 and 1991. The authors are grateful to the Czechoslovak authorities for their cooperation. The authors are also grateful to their colleagues Jeremy Carter, Nadeem Ul Haque, Kanitta Meesook, and Nissanke Weerasinghe, who contributed substantially to this study both directly and indirectly while working on the Czechoslovak team. The paper was edited by David Driscoll, Margaret Casey, and Elisa Diehl of the External Relations Department. The views expressed here, as well as any errors, are the sole responsibility of the authors and do not reflect the opinions of the IMF Executive Board or IMF staff.

The following symbols have been used throughout this paper:

... to indicate that data are not available;

— to indicate that the figure is zero or less than half the final digit shown, or that the item does not exist;

– between years or months (e.g., 1991–92 or January–June) to indicate the years or months covered, including the beginning and ending years or months;

/ between years (e.g., 1991/92) to indicate a crop or fiscal (financial) year.

"Billion" means a thousand million.

Minor discrepancies between constituent figures and totals are due to rounding.

The term "country," as used in this paper, does not in all cases refer to a territorial entity that is a state as understood by international law and practice; the term also covers some territorial entities that are not states, but for which statistical data are maintained and provided internationally on a separate and independent basis.

I Introduction

On December 10, 1989, it had been over forty years since the Communist party assumed control of the Czechoslovak Government, and over twenty years since the reforms of the "Prague Spring" failed. This was the legacy inherited by the new "Government of National Understanding," formed on that day, and by its successor, the democratically elected Government that took office in June 1990, which was virtually identical in composition to the interim Government it replaced. The economic legacy was shaped both by the distant past—Czechoslovakia's prewar history as a major industrial power—and by the recent past—slow economic decline under the Communist regime.

Before even its foundation as an independent state in 1918, and up to German occupation in 1938, Czechoslovakia had enjoyed a well-developed market system. By contrast, under the Communist regime, state control over the economy was more pervasive than elsewhere in Central and Eastern Europe. Almost all the means of production, including agriculture and small businesses, were in the hands of the state. The only significant physical asset in private hands was about half of the housing stock. Decisions relating to production, investment, and foreign trade were made by the state. Prices were centrally set, and wages tightly controlled. Efforts in the mid-1960s to reform this system, particularly by delegating decision making to enterprise management, were entirely reversed after 1968. Thus, although the market system survived as a dim memory, most skills associated with that system had faded by the 1980s.

Industry enjoyed a privileged position during the Communist era, and was relatively advanced by the 1980s, although plagued by inefficiency and outdated technology. Industrialization since 1948 had been guided both by the planners' preference for heavy industry and by the international division of labor within the Council for Mutual Economic Assistance (CMEA), which was only loosely related to Czechoslovakia's comparative advantage in a worldwide setting. Consequently, the economy had become extremely vulnerable to the terms of trade shock attendant on the collapse of the CMEA in January 1991.

The integration of Czechoslovakia into the world economy and the accommodation of the (long stifled) expression of its citizens' preferences call for a drastic change in production patterns. The country's industrial legacy affects this change in several ways. On the one hand, Czechoslovakia is endowed with a well-educated and skilled work force; it has also been left with a sizable stock of capital, at least some of which is usable in the new environment. These factors augur well for the success of reform in the longer term. On the other hand, Czechoslovakia's highly processed products are geared to specific needs and markets, and their redesign will require expertise, investment, and time. Thus, in the short run, Czechoslovakia's relatively advanced industrial structure can only complicate and slow the reorientation of production.

Finally, both in pre-Communist and Communist days, Czechoslovakia consistently implemented cautious macroeconomic management. Unlike other Central European countries, it did not experience runaway inflation in the 1920s.[1] During the Communist era, fiscal and credit policies were consistently conservative, and budgetary subsidies to enterprises were relatively small. Foreign debt was kept low, particularly compared to other centrally planned economies (Chart 1), and domestic imbalances were clearly smaller than in most centrally planned economies in the region. Recorded inflation was low, at an average of about $1^1/_2$ percent a year over the 1980s, and hidden inflation is thought to have amounted to no more than 3 percent a year. Moreover, both anecdotal evidence (the absence of pervasive shortages) and trends in the income velocity of money (which had declined only slightly during the 1980s) suggested that excess demand had not built up in the form of a large monetary overhang.

[1] A more complete historical background is provided by Prust and IMF Staff Team (1990) and Solimano (1991). For experiences with hyperinflation in the 1920s, see Dornbusch and Wolf (1990).

Chart 1. Comparative Foreign Debt Levels, 1989

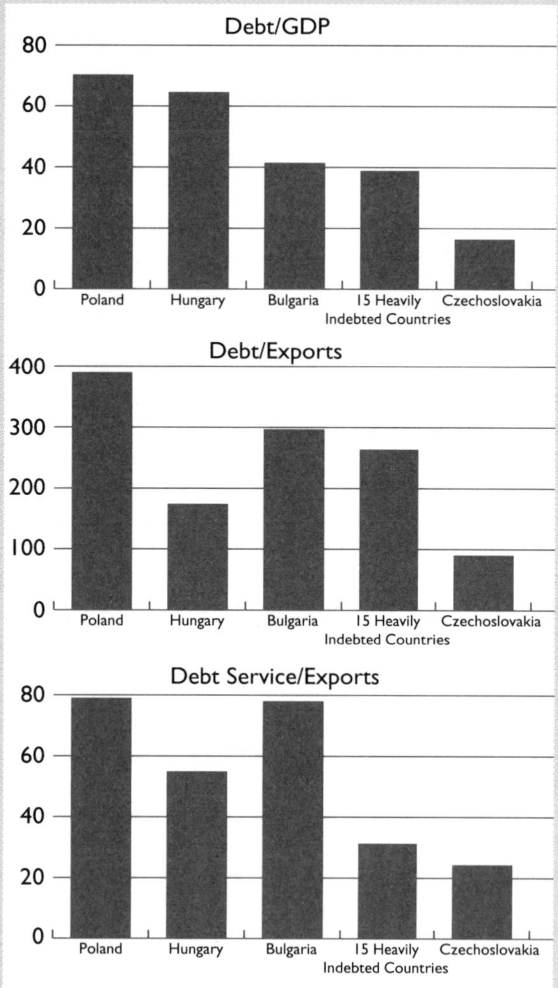

Sources: Country authorities; and IMF staff estimates.

From a macroeconomic point of view, therefore, Czechoslovakia enjoyed perhaps the best starting conditions for reform in Central and Eastern Europe—although the nearly complete domination of production by the state and virtual absence of any market mechanisms called for perhaps even more extensive structural reform than in the other planned economies. The Communist regime had initiated only a few cautious steps toward reform in late 1987. These included a small liberalization of the exchange and trade system aimed at encouraging exports in convertible currencies, a slight move toward greater enterprise autonomy, and a rationalization of wholesale prices, which continued to be administratively determined.

II Background to Reform

Preparations for reform began in earnest under the new Government in early 1990.[2] The interim Government acted quickly in several relatively uncontroversial areas, developing a comprehensive strategy of reform and building a consensus around it. Extensive discussions within the interim Government culminated in the adoption in May of a resolution setting forth a program of rapid reform, particularly in price and trade liberalization. This resolution was subsequently endorsed by the new Government, formed following the June elections, and the program was further elaborated in the "Scenario of Economic Reform," submitted to Parliament in September, which outlined "a comprehensive set of measures involving price liberalization, liberalization of imports and internal convertibility [that is, unrestricted access by businesses to foreign exchange for current account transactions], promotion of the growth of the private sector, macroeconomic anti-inflationary policy and the policy of social guarantees and social protection." A target date of January 1, 1991 was set for launching the radical phase of the reform program.

Policy Measures in 1990

In 1990, various preparatory measures were put in place. The new Government allowed two measures that had been prepared under the previous regime to come into force on January 1, 1990. First, a two-tier banking system was created by breaking up the State Bank; as an adjunct to the new banking structure, a discount rate was established—initially at 4 percent—for banks seeking to refinance. Second, a mixed system of centralized and decentralized prices was introduced. Under the new system, prices ranged from centrally determined to "contract prices," but even in the latter case prices remained subject to central intervention, so that in practice 1990 saw very little price liberalization.

[2]For further insight on the preliminary steps for economic reform, see Dyba and Svejnar (1991) and Klaus (1990).

The new Government also acted quickly to signal the new orientation of macroeconomic policy by declaring the need for fiscal and monetary austerity. The 1990 state budget, prepared under the previous Government, was withdrawn, and a new, tighter budget was presented, which showed a surplus of $^1/_2$ of 1 percent of GDP. At the same time, tight credit ceilings were imposed on the commercial banks. In addition, the new Government took a first step toward addressing the foreign exchange imbalance. The commercial and noncommercial exchange rates for the koruna were unified on January 8, 1990, at a level of Kcs 17 per U.S. dollar, representing sizable depreciations of both rates. A "tourist" exchange rate was also introduced, at a still more depreciated level.

Although prices remained essentially controlled throughout 1990, the new Government took steps to address some of the most glaring price distortions. On July 9, armed with the public mandate it had received from the elections, the Government raised retail food prices by an average of 25 percent, so as to eliminate retail subsidies amounting to over 3 percent of GDP. The population was compensated for these price increases by monthly income transfers of Kcs 140 (close to 5 percent of the average wage) a person. Some further administrative price adjustments, notably in transportation, were implemented in the following months to reduce subsidies even more.

A second set of crucial price adjustments was also initiated in July, this time in response to adverse external developments. As a result of the deepening economic crisis in the former U.S.S.R., the source of almost all its oil imports, Czechoslovakia was forced to purchase oil on the world market, at prices that were then inflated by the Middle East crisis. In an effort to reduce consumption, the retail prices of gasoline and diesel were raised between July and October, eventually to double their levels of early 1990. In effect, as far as retail prices of gasoline and diesel were concerned, the price adjustments that would be made necessary by the collapse of the CMEA in January 1991 had been completed in advance.

Table 1. Selected Economic and Financial Indicators

	1987	1988	1989	1990	First Half 1991 Estimated
Real sector (change in percent)					
Real GDP	2.1	2.5	1.4	–0.4	–9.2
Consumer prices					
Period average	0.1	0.2	2.3	10.8	. . .
End period	0.1	0.6	1.5	18.4	49.1
Industrial wholesale prices					
Period average	0.1	—	–0.7	4.4	. . .
End period	. . .	. . .	–0.7	16.6	53.3
Public finance (percent of GDP)					
General government[1]					
Revenue	57.9	58.0	62.1	60.2	47.4[2]
Expenditure[3]	58.7	59.5	64.5	60.1	46.7[2]
Surplus/deficit[3]	–0.7	–1.5	–2.4	–0.1	0.8[2]
Money and credit (end period, percent change)					
Net domestic assets	6.5	10.5	1.1	4.7	6.5
Credit to enterprises and households	3.3	3.1	–2.7	1.4	13.1
Broad money	6.0	11.5	3.5	0.5	5.6
Interest rates (percent)					
Credit to enterprises and cooperatives	5.1	5.1	5.7	6.5	19.5
Household savings deposits	4.0	4.0	4.0	4.3	13.0
Balance of payments (billion U.S. dollars)[4]					
Merchandise exports	15.7	15.1	14.3	11.7	4.7
CMEA	9.6	9.0	7.8	5.7	1.6
Other	6.1	6.1	6.5	6.0	3.1
Merchandise imports	15.8	14.7	14.0	13.2	5.0
Trade balance	–0.1	0.3	0.2	–1.5	–0.3
Current account	0.8	1.5	0.3	–1.3	—
Gross international reserves of the banking system (end of period)	1.5	1.7	2.3	1.2	1.7
In months of following-year imports in convertible currencies	3.6	4.2	4.9	1.2	. . .

Sources: Czechoslovak authorities; and IMF staff estimates.

[1]Includes federation and republics, local authorities, and extrabudgetary funds. Excludes National Property Funds, subsidized organizations, and funds of the ministries. Data for 1989 and 1990 are consistent with the *Government Finance Statistics* methodology.

[2]Revised budget for 1991.

[3]Excluding stock adjustments (mainly takeover of export credits and transfers to the banks on account of devaluation profits and losses).

[4]Transactions with former CMEA members in transferable rubles before 1991 converted at cross rates.

As the year progressed and the strategy of radical reform took shape, expectations of inflation and of devaluation spread—the latter boosted by some open discussion of various devaluation options in the Scenario of Economic Reform. The discount rate was raised to reach 8.5 percent by the end of the year, while deposit rates rose to 7–14 percent and lending rates to 15–22.5 percent. These moves, however, did not stanch the hemorrhaging of foreign exchange in anticipation of devaluation, as enterprises stocked up on imports and prepaid debt by any means available. On October 15, the commercial exchange rate was devalued by a further 35 percent, to Kcs 24 per U.S. dollar.

Throughout 1990, considerable efforts were also devoted to laying the legislative and institutional basis for the establishment and growth of a market economy in general and of private enterprise in particular. Among the most important legislative changes, a law on private enterprise was adopted allowing private sector participation in virtually any economic activity, the monopoly of foreign trade corporations on external trade was abolished, and the joint venture law was amended to allow for 100 percent foreign ownership. In addition, much of the planning apparatus was dismantled, the process of restructuring state enterprises into smaller and more independent joint stock companies was begun, and steps were taken to develop indirect instruments of monetary management.

The economic situation in 1990 was dominated by deepening difficulties in trade with the former U.S.S.R. and with other former CMEA countries undergoing adjustment and by the response to the very first steps of reform (Table 1). Net material product is estimated to have fallen by 3 percent, and the balance of payments to have deteriorated substantially, leaving gross international reserves at the end of the year equivalent to just over one month of imports. Consumer prices rose by 18 percent over the course of the year, largely as a result of the administrative price adjustments; producer prices, which toward the end of the year were permitted to adjust to reflect part of the impact of the October devaluation, rose only slightly less. The Government recorded a surplus of approximately 1 percent of GDP,[3] and, despite the substantial price increases, credit to the nongovernment sector rose by only about 1½ percent over the course of the year.

External Environment

The launching of the radical reform phase on January 1, 1991 was to coincide to the day with a major deterioration of the external environment associated with the shift in trade arrangements among the members of the former CMEA to pricing at world market prices and to settlement in convertible currencies. Evaluated at cross-exchange rates, CMEA trade accounted traditionally for over half of Czechoslovakia's exports and imports.[4] The shift to world prices represented both a large inflationary impulse and a major terms of trade shock, while the shift to convertible currencies would inhibit exports.

Up to 1990, almost all trade with the CMEA was denominated in transferable rubles. Prices in transferable rubles did bear some relation—discussed more fully below—to world prices, but this relation was based on the official exchange rate of the transferable ruble against the U.S. dollar, of TR 1 = US$1.60 (known as the IBEC exchange rate, for the Moscow-based International Bank for Economic Cooperation). Against the Czechoslovak koruna, on the other hand, the transferable ruble was valued at Kcs 9, equivalent on average in 1990 to $0.50 and after the December devaluation of the koruna to only $0.32. Abstracting from disparities between old transferable ruble prices and world prices, therefore, the abolition of the transferable ruble would have meant a fivefold increase in koruna prices of CMEA imports and exports.[5]

In addition, the move to world prices worsened Czechoslovakia's external terms of trade. Czechoslovakia's imports from the CMEA consisted mainly of raw materials and energy, and its exports to the CMEA mainly of capital goods and other manufactured products. Within the CMEA, the pricing systems for these two types of goods were different: prices of raw materials (at the IBEC exchange rate) were explicitly linked to a moving average of recent world prices, through the so-called Bucharest formula, whereas prices of manufactured goods were set on the basis of bilateral negotiations. Over time, the relative prices of manufactured goods had risen. In Czechoslovakia, it was estimated that—with transferable rubles converted into U.S. dollars at the IBEC rate—the move to world prices would reduce the dollar prices of imports from the CMEA by perhaps 5 percent and the dollar prices of exports to the CMEA by about 25 percent. As a result, the terms of trade with the CMEA would deteriorate by over 20 percent. The estimated terms of trade developments are plotted in Chart 2.

With the shift to settlement in convertible currencies, Czechoslovak products stood to lose an important advantage that they had enjoyed in competing for CMEA markets with products from other countries. This loss of competitiveness put additional pressure on export prices. Moreover, the clearing system had been instrumental in sustaining trade flows within the CMEA, as shortages of foreign exchange were felt throughout the region—most notably in the former U.S.S.R.—and the abolition of the clearing system thus brought with it the risk of a decline in export volumes. Exports to the former U.S.S.R. were likely to decline in any event as a result of the economic crisis in that country, and exports to the other former CMEA members would also come under pressure as economic reform and adjustment cut into these countries' ability to import.

For a time, it seemed that the rise in international oil prices owing to the Middle East crisis would further worsen the difficult external environment in which Czechoslovakia was determined to embark on its radical reform program. The fall in oil prices in early 1991 removed this aggravating

[3]Abstracting from certain stock adjustments relating to export credits to the former U.S.S.R. and to devaluation losses of the banks.

[4]As discussed below, the use of cross rates underestimates the weight of the CMEA in total trade.

[5]This comparison assumes that the exchange rate of the transferable ruble against the koruna would otherwise have remained unchanged; another counterfactual would yield a smaller impact of the abolition of the transferable ruble, but a larger impact of the devaluation of the koruna.

Chart 2. Terms of Trade

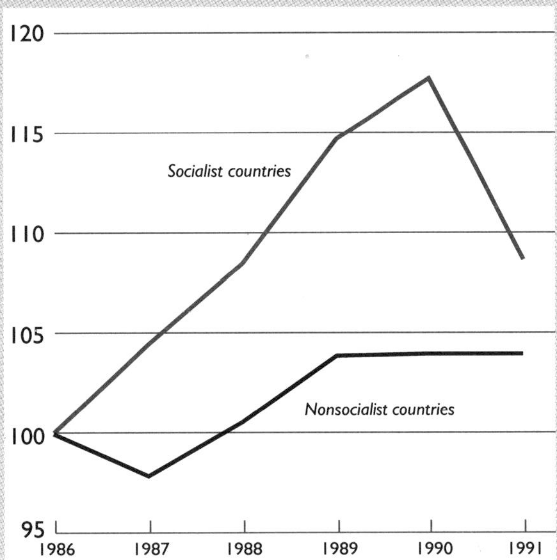

Sources: Czechoslovak authorities; and IMF staff estimates.

circumstance. Nevertheless, the collapse of the CMEA and the contraction of some of its major export markets were sufficient to present Czechoslovakia, for the first time in years, with a need for a serious stabilization effort, at the very same time that the crucial phase of reform was being launched.

The unfavorable external circumstances at the time the reform program was launched were bound to complicate further the transition to a market economy.[6] However, the advance setting of January 1, 1991 as a fixed and nonnegotiable deadline for launching the program was instrumental in coalescing the political forces and pushing through the necessary reforms without delay. Without the strong commitment to a specific date, pressures might have mounted regarding details not yet worked out, thereby delaying or even stalling the reform process.

[6]It is interesting to note that the unfavorable external environment itself was to a large extent a part of a wider trend to economic reform—the collapse of the CMEA being an integral part of the reform of the former centrally planned system, and the loss of export markets being due in part to reform efforts in neighboring countries.

III Reform Program of 1991

The comprehensive reform program that was implemented on January 1, 1991 comprised a major liberalization of domestic prices and of external trade and a rapid privatization program following an initial preparatory phase. The very unfavorable external environment made it even more pressing to proceed promptly with the reform measures but, at the same time, worsened the prospects for inflation and the balance of payments. To minimize the risk of financial instability in the critical initial phase of reform, the structural policies were supported by a mutually reinforcing package of financial policies comprising a pegged exchange rate and restrictive fiscal, monetary, and wage policies.

Policy-Sequencing Problem

The extent of the economic reforms to be undertaken raised an important issue of strategy, namely, the order in which the multiple reforms should be implemented.[7] Does it make sense to free markets (to liberalize prices and foreign trade), while production and trade are still in the hands of a few monopolistic state enterprises? Should price and trade liberalization be attempted simultaneously, or should the opening to foreign trade be postponed until enterprises are in a stronger competitive position?

For the most part, the answers to these questions derived not from advantages to be obtained by following a particular sequencing strategy, but instead from major economic and technical roadblocks—in the way of alternative paths. Postponing market liberalization until privatization had been completed would have implied a major delay in launching the reform process. For largely technical reasons, it is virtually impossible to transfer a major part of the state enterprise sector to private control in less than two or three years. The problem with this delay is that the intervening period could witness a major economic collapse, as the economy would find itself in a "no-man's-land" in which the central planning system has lost its ability to function (even at its normally poor level of efficiency), but new market-oriented initiatives are choked by price controls and economic restrictions. The situation in the former Soviet Union in the past few years, with its breakdown of traditional economic relations and multiplication of shortages, exemplifies the perils of delay. Moreover, this kind of sequencing would further complicate the sale of public enterprises, because their true market value would be even more difficult to assess; even a short experience under liberalized markets can provide some basis for evaluating the potential profitability of state enterprises.

Several considerations are germane to the question of whether foreign trade liberalization and the introduction of limited currency convertibility should be postponed in order to give enterprises more time to adjust. First, a staggering of price and trade liberalization entails successive waves of relative price adjustments, with each wave imposing additional adjustment costs on enterprises—involving, for example, investments, personnel, and technical changes. By contrast, a simultaneous liberalization of prices and trade allows the new "equilibrium" relative prices to be established quickly, thus minimizing the adjustment costs. Second, a postponement of trade liberalization would risk the creation of vested interests—for example, in import-competing sectors—that could make the process of opening up the economy politically more difficult. Finally, foreign trade liberalization is the only way of rapidly injecting substantial competition into a severely monopolized system and of avoiding abuses of market power. In so doing, trade liberalization also allows international prices of traded goods to serve as guidelines for the adjustment of all domestic prices, and a fixed exchange rate can become a strong anchor to hold down domestic inflation.[8]

---

[7]See Calvo and Frenkel (1991a), Dornbusch (1991), and Fischer and Gelb (1991) for more general treatment of the sequencing problem in the Eastern European context.

[8]Conditions for a successful convertibility are discussed by Portes (1991) and—more specifically for the case of Czechoslovakia—by Hrnčíř and Klacek (1991).

Thus, it was considered that the only feasible strategy was to proceed to price and trade liberalization in a "big bang" fashion while imposing hard budget constraints on state enterprises and undertaking the process of privatization as rapidly as possible. Aggregate demand policies were designed to be on the tight side in order to ensure the success of stabilization and to enforce financial discipline on state enterprises. For the first time, state enterprises were to find that their very existence depended on maintaining a viable financial position. Price subsidies were kept to a minimum, and a strengthened—though broad, in the absence of adequate targeting mechanisms—social safety net used instead to alleviate the effect of price increases on the lowest-income segments of the population. Foreign exchange was made freely available to businesses for their current account transactions, and direct restrictions and barriers to trade were minimized. Under these conditions, price and performance signals would begin to function as indicators of the potential market value of enterprises, facilitating their privatization.

Price Liberalization

A cornerstone of structural change in Czechoslovakia was the liberalization of prices, which had been administratively set for the previous forty years. On January 1, 1991, prices of goods and services representing about 85 percent of the total value of sales were freed, both at the producer and retail levels. Prices of public utilities, transport, and rents remained under regulation, as did a few products of vital importance, such as medicines (these items accounted for 6–8 percent of total turnover in the economy). In addition, temporary price guidelines were introduced for a list of specified goods, such as foodstuffs and intermediate goods of critical importance, in order to discourage speculative price rises. The concern was that in the absence of established competition and traditions of price setting, the monopolistic structure of many industries could lead to unwarranted price increases in the period immediately following the liberalization. These temporary price guidelines were eliminated by November 1991.

The liberalization of prices was reinforced by the removal of consumer subsidies. Following the earlier removal of retail subsidies on food, subsidies on industrial products were eliminated on January 1, 1991. After an initial postponement, subsidies on almost all energy products were eliminated in May 1991; as a result, coal prices rose by 240 percent, gas prices by 100 percent, and heating rates by 320 percent. Partial compensation for these price increases was granted to pensioners and families with children in the form of monthly income support of Kcs 80 a person (about 2 percent of the average wage). Thus, budgetary subsidies, which as recently as in 1989 had amounted to about 16 percent of GDP, were reduced to about 7 percent of GDP. Among the remaining items were agricultural subsidies (amounting to about 3 percent of GDP), partly to support minimum producer prices for a number of products; transport subsidies (a little over 1 percent of GDP) for the railway, intercity road transport, and urban transport; housing subsidies (about 1 percent of GDP) for maintenance of state-owned rental apartments and for low-interest loans; and small subsidies to oil- and gas-fired heating plants, which are more costly to operate but less damaging to the environment than the coal-fired plants.

The price structure was expected to change drastically in early 1991, not only because of the liberalization and the continued reduction in subsidies, but also because of external factors, including changes in the CMEA trading arrangements and the rise in the international price of oil. As a result of these external factors—which would raise prices of some raw material imports by as much as 300 percent—as well as the devaluation, prices of tradable goods were expected to rise substantially in early 1991. A precise quantification of the once-and-for-all impact of these external factors was impossible, but rough calculations suggested that, at a minimum, they would raise the price level by 25 percent. In addition, prices of goods that had been in short supply under central planning were expected to rise.

An important challenge in the early stage of reform was to ensure that the initial jump in prices did not give rise to an inflationary spiral. The formulation of fiscal and monetary policies was therefore based on the very conservative targets of limiting the initial price jump to 25 percent and the subsequent underlying inflation in the remainder of the year to an annual rate of 5 percent. These targets were clearly ambitious, even allowing for the absence of a major monetary overhang, such as that observed in the other centrally planned economies. But it was recognized that an overestimation of the initial price jump in the formulation of fiscal and monetary policies could in fact become self-fulfilling. Of course, aggregate demand policies based on an underestimated initial price increase could adversely affect economic activity, but it would be far easier to take corrective action in such a case than to err in the other direction and be forced to control runaway inflation or a balance of payments crisis in the midst of a program of fundamental structural reform.

Exchange and Trade Liberalization

The opening of the economy to international competition was the second cornerstone of the reform program. In order to infuse competition and bring the domestic price structure into line with international prices, virtually all restrictions on businesses' current account transactions were removed on January 1, 1991, while a full foreign exchange surrender requirement was imposed. Capital account transactions remained subject to control to minimize the risk of destabilizing capital outflows, particularly in view of the limited level of foreign reserves. Under the new system, the annual foreign exchange plan was abandoned, and trade activities by all registered businesses (state or private) were freely allowed. Only a few strategic imports remained subject to import licensing. Subsequently, profits and dividends were made fully remittable (in February), and the annual entitlement to foreign exchange for individuals traveling abroad was raised to Kcs 5,000 from Kcs 2,000 (in April). In addition, the system of levies and subsidies, which bridged differences between domestic and international prices, was abolished on January 1, as was the export premium scheme, which subsidized exports to the convertible currency area. Export-licensing requirements on a large number of products were removed.

An important adjunct to trade reform was the dismantling of the CMEA trade and payments arrangements. Effective January 1, 1991, trade with CMEA members was to be conducted on the basis of world prices and payments to become due in convertible currencies, replacing bilateral and multilateral arrangements. However, already prior to that date and increasingly as 1991 progressed, it was evident that trade within the CMEA was in danger of collapsing on the new basis; exports to the former Soviet Union, in particular, appeared to be hardly feasible on a convertible currency basis because importers were unable to secure the necessary foreign exchange. To avoid the loss of these markets, which, owing to the specificity of most manufactured exports, would be difficult to replace in the short run, some temporary arrangements were necessary. These took the form initially of dollar-denominated clearing arrangements under which goods on the "indicative lists"—which defined areas of trade of mutual benefit—could be traded; later in 1991 a framework for clearing accounts denominated in national currencies was also created.

With the liberalization of imports, there was concern that pent-up demand for consumer goods might lead to a surge in imports in early 1991. Thus, in order to contain pressures on international reserves, the authorities imposed, on a temporary basis, a 20 percent surcharge on virtually all imports of consumer goods. This surcharge was reduced to 15 percent by mid-1991 and is likely to be eliminated in the near future in conjunction with a planned restructuring of the tariff system. Since the planning system relied on the foreign exchange plan to regulate imports and protect domestic industries, the present tariffs are generally low, averaging about 5 percent. The authorities have accordingly decided to review and modify the tariff structure beginning in 1992, with a view to providing domestic industries with appropriate protection, in particular in light of subsidies given by some neighboring countries to the agricultural sector.[9]

Foreign investment has been promoted in the context of the structural reform in general, and the privatization program in particular. The Joint Ventures Act, as amended in 1990, together with the Foreign Exchange Act, has established a framework for joint ventures and foreign-owned companies, under which these companies could be subject to less restrictive regulations than those applicable to domestic enterprises regarding foreign exchange accounts abroad and borrowing from foreign banks. In addition, foreign investors may freely repatriate capital. Moreover, bilateral agreements that would guarantee even more favorable conditions for foreign investors have been reached or are under negotiation with most western industrial countries.

Exchange Rate Policy and Reserve Management

A critical aspect of the stabilization program was the choice between a flexible or a pegged exchange rate, which raised a number of issues. Under a flexible regime, the determination of the level of the exchange rate would be left to market forces. Such a regime entailed substantial risk, however, given the absence of an established foreign exchange market, as well as the substantial uncertainty relating to changes in both the price structure and the trade patterns in the aftermath of price and trade liberalization. A major concern was that, under those circumstances, a freely floating system would be very fragile, and the initial price jump or an initial surge in imports would trigger a vicious circle of sharp speculative depreciation of the koruna,

[9]In July 1991, pending this tariff restructuring, the Government imposed temporary import quotas on certain agricultural products, in order to stem subsidized imports from neighboring countries.

domestic inflation, and accompanying wage increases. The risk of speculative attacks on the koruna was heightened by the low level of international reserves. The uncertainty relating to the extent of intervention necessary to stabilize the exchange rate, as well as the authorities' relative inexperience in managing a floating exchange rate, was expected to reduce the availability of foreign exchange resources from both official and private sources.[10]

Against this background, the authorities decided to unify the commercial and tourist exchange rates at a competitive level and to peg the rate to a basket of currencies of major partner countries in the West. The pegged rate, together with restrictive fiscal, monetary, and incomes policies, was designed to provide an effective anchor for stabilizing prices in the period following their liberalization. The commitment to a pegged rate was also expected to enhance the authorities' credibility in putting in place restrictive aggregate demand policies and therefore discourage speculative capital outflows. Furthermore, in the absence of futures markets or hedging facilities, a pegged regime would facilitate trade by reducing exchange rate volatility.

In order to ensure the viability of the pegged regime, it was critical that the initial exchange rate parity be set at a level that was both consistent with a sustainable current account position over the medium term and credible from a short-term perspective. In setting this rate, it was therefore necessary to anticipate a substantial erosion in external competitiveness in early 1991 owing to large domestic price increases of other origin, which were difficult to project accurately. This consideration, together with a precarious level of international reserves, dictated that any error in setting the exchange rate be on the side of overdepreciation. Although it was recognized that any such overdepreciation could by itself amplify the initial price increase, it was feared that a small devaluation would induce large capital outflows, given strong speculation by the public that the koruna would be devalued by a large amount. Accordingly, on December 28, 1990, the exchange rate of the koruna was set at Kcs 28 = US$1; this action represented a devaluation of the koruna (at the commercial rate) by about 15 percent, implying a total devaluation of over 45 percent during 1990 (Chart 3).

Notwithstanding the substantial devaluation of the koruna in 1990, it was recognized that a structural transformation could be attained only after a time lag and that, in the meantime, the trade and payments position was likely to deteriorate.[11] Thus, a sound financial program in the context of a pegged exchange rate required an adequate level of reserves at the outset. In this context, large-scale financial support from the IMF was indispensable. Access to IMF resources in the amount of up to $1.8 billion was provided under a stand-by arrangement and the compensatory and contingency financing facility. Of this amount, about $0.7 billion was disbursed in early January to boost the initial level of reserves to about one and a half months of imports. Support from the IMF provided a respite while other financial support could be arranged. Subsequently in 1991, commitments of about $1 1/2 billion were made by the European Community, the other industrial countries of the Group of 24, and the World Bank—of which about half is expected to be disbursed in 1991 and the remainder in 1992.

Chart 3. Exchange Rates
Koruny per U.S. dollar (end of period)

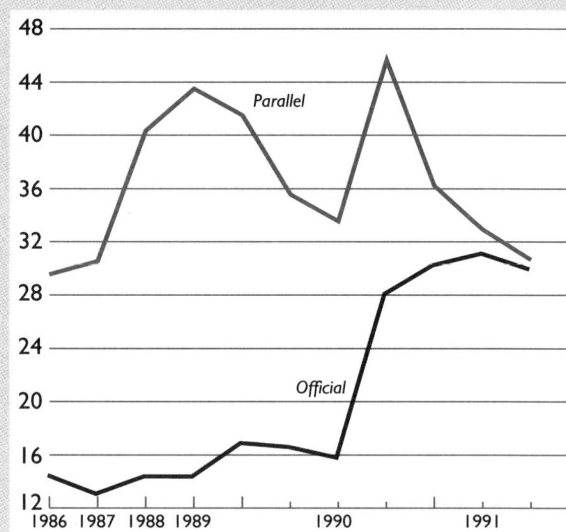

Sources: Czechoslovak authorities; and Schweizerischer Bankverein.

Fiscal Policy

Fiscal policy was designed to achieve two broad aims: to further the disengagement of the state from the economy and to help stabilize the econ-

[10]See Aghevli, Khan, and Montiel (1991) for general considerations on the choice of an exchange rate regime.

[11]The requirement of external support for reform programs is certainly a common feature in the formerly centrally planned economies. For a general assessment, see Collins and Rodrik (1991) and Diwan and Saldanha (1991).

omy in the turbulent period following the big bang and the terms of trade shock. With the former objective in mind, the rates of tax on profits were reduced by 10–20 percentage points and largely unified; the myriad rates of turnover tax (sales tax) were reduced to three (in addition to a zero rate); and, as explained above, subsidies were drastically reduced.[12]

To further the stabilization objective, fiscal policy for 1991 was aimed at an overall budget surplus of about 1 percent of GDP (Table 2).[13] The implied improvement of less than 1 percent of GDP in the budget balance (over 1990) substantially understated the adjustment effort. In particular, the ratio of revenue to GDP was—again conservatively—estimated to fall by about 10 percentage points, owing in part to policy decisions, but principally to exogenous factors, including the expected difficulties of enterprises and the projected fall in employment and real wages. Furthermore, proceeds from privatization were not to be included as budgetary revenues but were to be blocked in the accounts of the National Property Funds with the banks. Consequently, the envisaged budget surplus required considerable expenditure restraint. Even under the conservative target of a 30 percent price increase in 1991, all components of expenditure would decline substantially in real terms, lowering the ratio of government spending to GDP by about 11 percentage points. The most severe cuts fell on subsidies, and the least severe on the social safety net. Public investment, recognized to have a crucial role to play in the face of urgent infrastructural needs, was cut only slightly more than government consumption expenditure.

The fiscal stance in early 1991 was substantially tighter than envisaged, reflecting a temporary surge in profit tax receipts owing mainly to capital gains on inventories (high penalties on late payment of taxes—of ½ of 1 percent a day—ensured that tax payments ranked among enterprises' highest priorities). In addition, expenditures were deliberately limited with a view to bolstering the anti-inflationary stance in the crucial first few months of the year; thus pensions and government wages were increased with a significant lag following the price jump, and payments over which the Government had discretion—notably subsidies and capital transfers—were postponed. Altogether, the overall budget surplus in the first quarter amounted to about 2½ percent of (annual) GDP.[14]

The exceptionally strong fiscal performance of the first quarter was not expected to endure. In particular, most sources of revenue were expected to be adversely affected by the economic decline, while government spending relating to the social safety net would increase owing to the rise in unemployment. In addition, expenditure allocations for some sensitive services (notably health and education) had to be revised upward as a result of the higher-than-expected price jump, but this revision was not approved until July. In light of very weak domestic demand, the authorities were concerned that the unwinding of the tight fiscal stance might be too slow. Thus, to give both a signal and an immediate boost to domestic demand, the rates of turnover tax were lowered by 1–3 percentage points in mid-1991.

Expectations of a turnaround in the fiscal position were confirmed in the third quarter. After a small additional surplus in the second quarter, the Government recorded a deficit of about 1 percent of (annual) GDP in the third quarter. As the windfall gain on the profits tax subsided, all the major sources of revenue began to show the effects of declining economic activity, and the lags in expenditures began to unwind. For the year as a whole, the overall fiscal position is expected to be broadly balanced—somewhat weaker than originally budgeted, as the effects of the sharp drop in activity offset the initial windfall gain on the profits tax. With the revision of expenditure allocation in July, nominal spending exceeded the original budget but, in real terms, the spending cuts were significantly larger than originally envisaged. This tight fiscal stance has proved instrumental in checking price rises and alleviating pressures on the balance of payments, although it has inevitably contributed to the weakening of domestic demand. It should be noted, however, that the dependence of the 1991 fiscal results on the windfall gain on the profits tax and on favorable lags foreshadows the even greater challenge that will face the authorities in maintaining an appropriately anti-inflationary fiscal stance in 1992.

Monetary Policy

Monetary policy, like fiscal policy, was designed to be restrictive so as to bolster the exchange rate anchor and help stabilize prices. A tight credit policy was intended to ensure that the initial price

[12]As in other socialist economies, the tax system in Czechoslovakia was highly distortionary, with extremely high profit tax rates. See Tanzi (1991).

[13]The overall budget comprises the budgets of the Federal Government, the two republics, and the local authorities, as well as extrabudgetary operations. It does not include operations of the National Property Funds, to which the proceeds from privatization accrue.

[14]All references to the fiscal balance in 1991 exclude certain stock adjustments that were carried out to adjust the distribution of assets and liabilities between the Government and other parts of what was formerly the state. These are listed in Table 2.

Table 2. Fiscal Operations

	1990[1]	1991 Budget	1991 Jan.–June Actual[2]	1991 Revised Budget[3]	1991 Jan.–Sept. Actual[2]
	(In billions of koruny)				
Central government (federation and republics)					
Revenue	399.2	403.1	220.1	482.5	344.8
Individual income taxes	0.3	39.8	18.2	56.1	40.7
Profits taxes	93.4	91.7	81.3	136.8	105.1
Payroll tax[4]	81.4	90.1	34.2	107.2	70.1
Taxes on goods and services	147.8	154.3	63.5	141.9	91.7
Taxes on international trade	25.8	8.0	5.4	8.8	8.5
Other	50.5	19.2	17.5	31.7	28.5
Expenditure and net lending	387.6	395.1	203.0	478.5	340.0
Current transfers	248.1	216.2	109.0	297.5	206.9
To enterprises and cooperatives	103.2	44.8	25.7	64.6	45.3
To subsidized organizations	3.2	4.5	2.0	11.4	5.5
To local authorities	33.4	9.8	10.5	63.0	44.2
To households	108.3	157.2	70.7	158.4	111.8
Unemployment benefit and retraining	—	9.8	1.2	9.8	2.3
General income support	12.7	32.9	12.8	32.0	. . .
Other	95.6	114.5	56.7	116.6	. . .
Other current expenditure	86.5	139.5	76.8	138.2	102.1
Capital expenditure	7.2	16.0	4.8	14.3	8.3
Capital transfers	45.1	27.6	12.9	33.2	20.2
To local authorities	30.2	14.1	8.2	15.2	11.9
Other	14.8	13.5	4.7	18.0	8.3
Net lending	0.7	–4.3	–0.5	–4.7	2.5
Surplus/deficit	11.6	8.0	17.1	4.0	4.8
Stock adjustments[5]	–54.4	—	16.9	13.9	16.9
Adjustment for complementary period[6]	–9.8	—	8.2	5.5	5.7
Local authorities	–0.9	—	3.1	—	7.9
Revenue	162.4	86.2	54.3	95.6	. . .
Of which: transfers from central government	63.6	23.9	18.7	78.1	56.1
Expenditure	163.3	86.2	51.2	95.6	. . .
Extrabudgetary funds	–0.2	—	0.3	—	0.6
Overall surplus/deficit	–53.7	8.0	45.6	24.9	36.0
Excluding stock adjustments	0.7	8.0	28.7	8.0	19.1

Sources: Czechoslovak authorities; and IMF staff estimates.

[1]Figures for 1990 are not comparable with those for 1991 because of changes in the division of revenues and expenditures between central and local government.

[2]Revenue and expenditure adjusted for off-budget transactions.

[3]Methodological changes compared to the original budget consist of the transfer of certain own revenues of the local authorities (individual income taxes and payroll tax; full-year total Kcs 44.4 billion) to the central budget, with an equivalent increase in transfers to the local authorities; and the transfer of certain "other" current expenditures (full-year total Kcs 6.8 billion) to subsidized organizations.

[4]Nonfinancial state enterprises only.

[5]Includes transfers related to devaluation losses and profits of banks and foreign trade organizations and takeover of export credits.

[6]Adjusts the fiscal balance of central government from an accrual to a cash basis.

jump did not trigger a process of protracted inflation.

The velocity of broad money was expected to increase, reflecting the greater availability of nonmonetary assets, including consumer durables and equity obtained through the privatization of small-scale enterprises in early 1991 and of larger enterprises (albeit on a limited scale) later in the year. Thus, the monetary program had to allow for a shift in savings from monetary to real assets, which would reduce the demand for money. In line with the projected increase in velocity and the targeted balance of payments, the financial program envisaged a tight credit policy, particularly in the period immediately after the liberalization of prices (Table 3). The envisaged decline in net credit to the Government corresponding to the budget surplus, together with the expected proceeds from privatization (to be held by the National Property Funds), would provide adequate room to meet the credit needs of the nongovernment sector under the credit ceilings. In the event, the price jump turned out higher than anticipated, and the financial program was revised accordingly.

Credit policy was to be implemented mainly through direct ceilings on commercial banks. While such ceilings inevitably create inefficiencies and distortions, the rudimentary nature of financial markets made it impossible to rely on reserve money management and other indirect instruments. The State Bank, however, introduced a number of measures to move toward a system of reserve money management. These include the requirement that interbank accounts be settled in the State Bank's books—a prerequisite for state bank control over reserve money; a change in the reserve system to one based on an average monthly holding period to smooth the operation of the new interbank settlement system; and the introduction of reserve requirements and refinance auctions. The authorities intend to take further steps in this direction, including the introduction of a treasury or state bank bill, so as to allow for the implementation of monetary policy through market-based instruments. In addition, new banking laws are to be introduced, which should promote the independence of the State Bank and further the development of a competitive banking system (including through the entry of foreign banks).

As in the case of fiscal policy, credit conditions in early 1991 turned out to be considerably tighter than planned (Chart 4). Several factors appear to have constrained the supply of credit. On the technical side, the reliance on direct credit ceilings proved inefficient because margins not used by certain banks could not be used by other banks; furthermore, the State Bank and, in turn, head offices of commercial banks built significant safety margins into their ceilings. More fundamentally, the banks were reluctant to lend in the highly uncertain environment in view of the changing prospects facing enterprises and also of the banks' own inexperience in credit risk assessment. The deficiencies of the banks' balance sheets, owing to their low capital-asset ratios and their poor loan portfolios, compounded this reluctance to lend. With the encouragement of the State Bank and helped by the stabilization of the macroeconomic situation, credit picked up after the first quarter, but remained tight—as evidenced for instance by a sharp increase in interenterprise payment arrears. While the tight stance of credit policy, especially in the early months, helped avoid the onset of an inflationary spiral and of pressures in foreign exchange markets, it may have added to the weakness of aggregate demand and the contraction in output.

Debt Overhang of Enterprises

A major obstacle to an efficient functioning of the banking system has been the legacy of large amounts of bank credit extended to enterprises under government direction over many years, a situation described as the "soft budget constraint" (Kornai (1986)). A large portion of bank credits is of questionable value, as enterprises may not be in a position to repay them. These loans are not only burdensome to banks, but in some cases may financially choke enterprises that could be profitable on current operations, but that are saddled with large debts incurred through arbitrary price setting and investment decisions under central planning. From the point of view of banks, the carryover of these debts distorts the allocation of credit and increases the spread between deposit and lending rates. Moreover, given the weak capital and reserves position of commercial banks, this situation threatens the stability of the emerging financial system, highlighting the need both to put the commercial banks on a sound footing and to introduce proper prudential banking supervision.[15]

To the extent that bad debts are owed by enterprises that are not viable and need to be liquidated, the solution—recapitalization of the banks—is fairly clear cut. However, to the extent that the debt overhang also pertains to enterprises that are potentially profitable, it is not possible to devise a "clean" solution. A comprehensive auditing of banks and enterprises to identify the proper action in each individual case would take time and create serious moral hazard problems in the interim.

[15]See Calvo and Frenkel (1991b).

Table 3. Monetary Survey

	1989	1990	1991 March	1991 June	1991 Sept.
			(In billions of koruny)		
Net international reserves[1]	17.8	–4.3	–12.8	–9.6	–2.0
Foreign assets[2]	37.8	27.7	32.8	41.3	58.8
Foreign liabilities	20.0	32.0	45.6	50.9	60.8
Net domestic assets	530.0	555.0	558.5	593.5	628.1
Domestic credit	583.6	640.2	656.0	667.3	702.2
Net credit to government	5.9	54.2	37.9	8.6	18.2
Net credit to Property Funds	0.0	0.0	–0.9	–4.2	–11.7
Credit to enterprises and households	577.7	586.0	619.0	662.9	695.7
Credit to enterprises	530.8	536.0	567.8	611.3	642.6
Credit to households	46.9	50.0	51.2	51.6	53.1
Broad money	547.8	550.7	545.7	583.9	626.1
Money	311.1	291.2	279.9	294.3	324.7
Currency outside banks	68.0	73.7	72.9	76.2	80.7
Demand deposits	243.1	217.5	207.0	218.1	244.0
Households	107.5	103.3	95.7	92.0	92.0
Enterprises[3]	135.6	114.2	111.3	126.1	152.0
Quasi money	236.7	259.5	265.8	289.6	301.4
Time and savings deposits	232.5	231.7	240.2	254.0	259.1
Households	170.2	167.4	171.3	180.1	188.1
Enterprises[3]	62.3	64.3	68.9	73.9	71.0
Foreign currency deposits[1]	4.2	27.8	25.6	35.6	42.3
Households	1.7	9.8	12.6	16.3	21.0
Enterprises[3]	2.5	18.0	13.0	19.3	21.3
Other items, net[4]	53.6	85.2	97.5	73.8	74.1
Memorandum items:			*(Change in percent of broad money at beginning of year)*		
Broad money	3.5	0.5	–0.9	6.0	13.7
Money	0.3	–3.6	–2.1	0.6	6.1
Quasi money	3.2	4.2	1.1	5.5	7.6
Net international reserves	2.6	–4.0	–1.5	–1.0	0.4
Net domestic assets	0.9	4.6	0.6	7.0	13.3
Domestic credit	7.7	10.3	2.9	4.9	11.3
Other items, net	–6.9	–5.8	–2.2	2.1	2.0

Sources: State Bank of Czechoslovakia; and IMF staff estimates.
[1]End of period. At current exchange rates through 1990, and at end-December 1990 rates for subsequent periods.
[2]Assets from 1990 are strictly comparable to international reserves at end-period exchange rate. Earlier data use state bank valuation of monetary gold.
[3]Including insurance companies.
[4]Including net nonconvertible assets and long-term assets of Obchodni Bank.

Moral hazard will also arise if, in an attempt to avoid overestimating the size of the problem in the face of a need for quick action, a debt-relief operation is conducted in installments, with no clear signal that it is the last such operation. Moreover, debt write-downs should target enterprises that have the greatest potential for improving their performance and increasing their investment, which means that very good and very bad enterprises should be excluded; the scheme should be carefully designed in this respect because, from the point of view of banks, it is debt write-offs for the worst enterprises that most help their balance sheets. Finally, not only will a debt-relief operation be complicated, but it will also be costly if it is to be comprehensive enough to have an impact on the

Chart 4. Nominal and Real Money Supply
(Index 1990:IV=100)

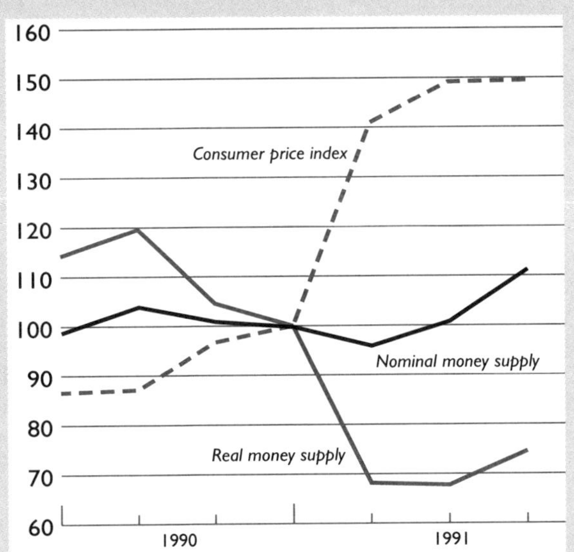

Source: Czechoslovak authorities.

performance of the economy. This cost, however, should not be overestimated. For enterprises that are to be privatized through direct sales, debt relief will presumably be reflected in higher sale prices. Moreover, to the extent that the authorities wish to protect deposit holders, the bad debt overhang already implies a financial liability for the state, albeit a contingent one. If enterprises are unable to repay banks, and banks become unable to repay depositors, it will be up to the state to cover the resource gap.

As a first step in addressing the banks' portfolio problems, measures were taken in March to carve out of the banks' balance sheets a large part of permanently revolving credits for inventories (TOZ credits). These credits, which had originally been extended at 6 percent interest and with no maturity date, were officially abolished at the beginning of 1991, but problems arose when banks and enterprises attempted to negotiate replacement loans with longer-term maturities and at commercial rates. A new agency, the Consolidation Bank, was created to take over the bulk of TOZ loans—some Kcs 110 billion, equivalent to almost one fifth of the stock of bank credit to enterprises—with eight-year maturities and at an interest rate of 13 percent (corresponding to its average cost of funds). On its liability side, the Consolidation Bank took over from the commercial banks a portion of their liabilities to the State Bank and of the deposits by the savings banks. By removing a number of questionable loans from commercial banks' portfolios, the establishment of the Consolidation Bank was a first step in the direction of improving the efficiency of the banking system. However, the operation was very partial, and a large number of nonperforming loans remained on banks' books. Moreover, the beneficial impact on both banks and enterprises was quite limited: banks gave up low-cost liabilities of a similar value, and, since no provisions were made for write-offs or write-downs, enterprises continued to carry TOZ debts on their books.

Further measures were undertaken in October 1991, when it was decided to transfer to the commercial banks Kcs 50 billion in bonds issued by the National Property Funds. Of this amount, Kcs 10–15 billion was earmarked for capitalization of the banks, thus providing some cushion against the effects of the inevitable bankruptcies. The rest was to be used to compensate banks for writing off loans of enterprises with large debts but good economic potential. Given the uncertainties surrounding estimates of the amount of bad and doubtful loans outstanding, it is not clear whether this operation alone will resolve the issue.

Interest Rate Policy

Czechoslovakia's financial markets are not adequately developed to generate autonomously a market-clearing interest rate. The banking system is still in an infant stage, besides being saddled with weak balance sheets and strong oligopolistic elements. Furthermore, the instruments and markets that would enable the central bank to manage conditions in financial markets are still in a rudimentary state. Thus, interest rate policy was to be designed fairly independently of the targets for domestic credit, albeit with a consideration not to worsen existing disequilibria in financial markets.

The first important issue was the determination of interest rates for the first few weeks of 1991, when prices were expected to jump sharply. Interest rates in the final months of 1990 had not been high enough to prevent large-scale hoarding and capital outflows in anticipation of devaluation and price increases, but with the price jump in early 1991, an entirely new scenario would unfold. Should one attempt to maintain, ex post, positive real interest rates, or should one set interest rates in a forward-looking way with reference only to the expected inflation—and other factors—after the price jump had taken place? The authorities chose the latter course of action for a number of reasons.

First, raising interest rates would do little to reduce the size of the price jump. As argued above, the price jump was essentially caused by a number of supply-side factors, such as the adjustment of raw material prices and of the exchange rate. On the demand side, interest rates would not affect significantly the behavior of consumers. On the one hand, purchases of what had been shortage goods would be unlikely to be reduced or postponed because of the opportunity of earning an ex post real interest rate of a few percentage points during January–February. On the other hand, with the widespread knowledge that prices would jump on and after January 1, purchases for purposes of stocking up would have been largely completed prior to that date; besides, expectations of inflation during the price jump could be low or even negative, as the public, who had little prior experience of inflation, might at any time after January 1 expect that the price jump had worked itself out or even overshot.

Second, unduly high interest rates would have a number of undesirable consequences. Higher interest costs, with widespread cost-plus pricing, would in fact magnify the price jump. A rise in interest rates to levels rarely seen in Western European countries could give a wrong signal that inflation would persist, thereby leading to ingrained inflationary expectations. Finally, a short period of ex post negative real interest rates would contribute to reducing the inherited high indebtedness of enterprises and to eliminating any existing monetary overhang.

Nevertheless, interest rates needed to be high enough to protect the balance of payments position. Although controls on capital flows were to remain in place, it was clear that, as elsewhere, these controls would not prevent large capital outflows should domestic assets not bear an appropriate premium. In this context, it was of course crucial that the entire economic program be credible, in particular, that the exchange rate be judged adequate to withstand the expected adjustment of prices. On the basis of these assumptions, a premium of a few percentage points over foreign interest rates was judged to be sufficient to make domestic deposits attractive, and interest rate policy was geared to this objective.

The problem of the weakness of banks' balance sheets posed an additional problem in the determination of appropriate lending interest rates. On the one hand, high lending rates would end up worsening the debt overhang problem for some enterprises and, more important, it would unjustly (and inefficiently) penalize all new investment projects for the "sins" of years of central planning. On the other hand, both the riskiness of loans to highly indebted enterprises and the weak financial position of banks called for relatively high lending rates. The permissible interest rate spread started relatively high, but was later narrowed in stages, reflecting mainly the authorities' concern over the oligopolistic structure of the banking system, and anticipating steps to remove doubtful loans from banks' portfolios. The reduction in the spread may, however, have made it more difficult for some of the riskier borrowers—including the emerging private sector—to get access to credit.

Although banks were formally granted some leeway in determining interest rates, the State Bank kept close control over rates with the aid of three instruments: the discount rate, a maximum lending rate, and moral suasion in the matter of deposit rates. The discount rate plays a large role in the determination of the banks' cost of funds because the large banks rely heavily on State Bank refinancing. Initially, the discount rate was set at 10 percent (somewhat above its level of 8½ percent at the end of 1990), the maximum lending rate at 14 percentage points above the discount rate, and the notional target for deposit rates at a few percentage points above the discount rate. One-year deposit rates settled in the range of 13–16 percent, with lending rates ranging from 17 percent to 24 percent (Chart 5). Apart from loan risk considerations, the high spread between deposit and lending rates reflected high costs associated with the inefficiency of the banks; the oligopolistic structure of the banking system contributed to keep lending rates close to their maximum authorized level. The maximum lending interest rate was later reduced in successive stages to 17 percent by September, and the discount rate was lowered to 9½ percent.

Developments in the first part of 1991 largely confirmed the validity of the assumptions on which Czechoslovakia's interest rate policy was built. There was no evidence of capital outflows on a significant scale. Foreign currency deposits rose only moderately, reflecting a sharp deceleration relative to the growth in this type of deposits during 1990.[16] In addition, interest rates did not unduly stimulate demand early in the year as both investment and consumer demand were in fact very weak during the first quarter.

Incomes Policy

An integral element of the anti-inflationary program was the containment of wage growth. To this end, the General Agreement concluded in January by the Government, employers, and trade unions established a cap on wage increases during 1991

[16]Foreign currency deposits of enterprises remained at about their level of December 1990, but were constrained by the new foreign exchange surrender requirements.

Chart 5. One-year Interest Rate[1]

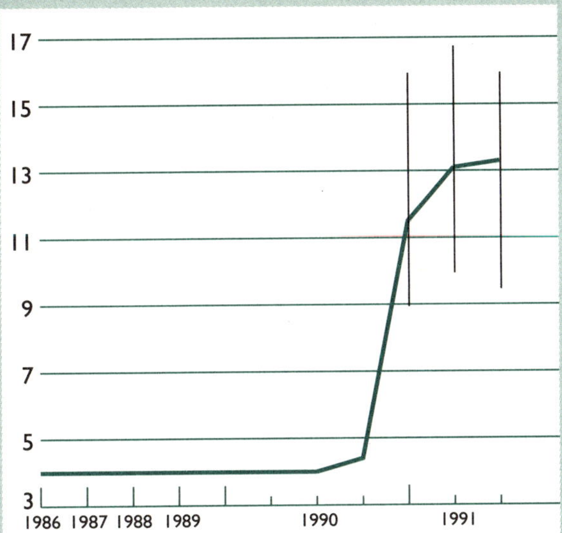

Source: Czechoslovak authorities.
[1]One-year deposit rate.

consistent with a decline in real wages of 10 percent compared with December 1990—following an earlier decline of about 10 percent over the course of 1990. Wage increases in excess of this guideline would be penalized by prohibitive taxation of enterprises (the so-called excess wage tax), except in the case of those with fewer than 25 employees.

In practice, wage increases were contained well below the levels permitted by the General Agreement, reflecting the unfavorable financial position of enterprises and the weak bargaining power of labor in an environment of rising unemployment. Nominal wages in the second quarter are estimated to have been some 12 percent above their level at the end of 1990, implying a fall of over 20 percent in real terms (Chart 6). In the wake of these deep cuts, nominal wages were expected to increase somewhat during the remainder of 1991, but they should remain well within the agreed guidelines.

Also as part of the General Agreement, a minimum wage of Kcs 2,000 a month was established in January—well above the previously existing lowest wages in the economy. The authorities are concerned that this minimum wage may contribute to the rise in unemployment and have resisted pressures for its indexation.

The wage restraint policy has served two important objectives. The first and more immediate objective has been to contain inflationary tendencies arising from the jump in prices that followed their liberalization. But a second important objective is to reinforce other efforts to strengthen financial discipline and to preclude excessive wage increases by state enterprises, particularly those with uncertain prospects. The current excess wage tax virtually excludes the whole emerging private sector because it does not apply to enterprises with fewer than 25 employees, and the Government is considering explicitly exempting all private sector firms from the excess wage tax in the near future.

Privatization

Privatization is the most challenging and, perhaps, the most critical of the economic reforms being undertaken. Czechoslovakia finds itself in the tenuous situation in which the central planning system has been dismantled, but the lack of widespread private property and of a clear profit motive places it some distance from a full-fledged market system. State enterprises account for virtually all economic activity. Their managers are unfamiliar with and untrained for a market system; moreover, their perception of a highly uncertain tenure creates perverse incentives for excessive wage and bonus payments, low investment, and squandering of the assets of the enterprises.

Compared with the divestment of large enterprises, the privatization of small enterprises is relatively simple, and began in January 1991. The "small privatization" program consists of sales of small businesses through auctions in which all resident Czechoslovak citizens can participate and for which bank financing has been provided. Auctions are being held as often as four times a week throughout the country and over 20,000 small enterprises—mainly but not exclusively retail outlets—had already been privatized by this method by November. Small enterprises are generally sold without their debts, which are repaid out of the proceeds of the auctions; but in a number of auctions held later in the year, some enterprises (typically somewhat larger ones) were sold with their liabilities. In addition, large numbers of small enterprises, which were expropriated after 1948, are being returned to their previous owners.

As regards privatization of larger enterprises, the authorities were determined to proceed at once, even at the risk of difficulties arising from the sheer scale of the effort and the lack of adequate expertise and developed markets, lest the inefficiency of the system of public enterprise management and control blunt the progress of all reforms. But the question was how to proceed with privatization. It was recognized that conventional sale methods could have only a limited role for a number of reasons, including the near impossibility of obtaining a

Chart 6. Average Employee Compensation[1]

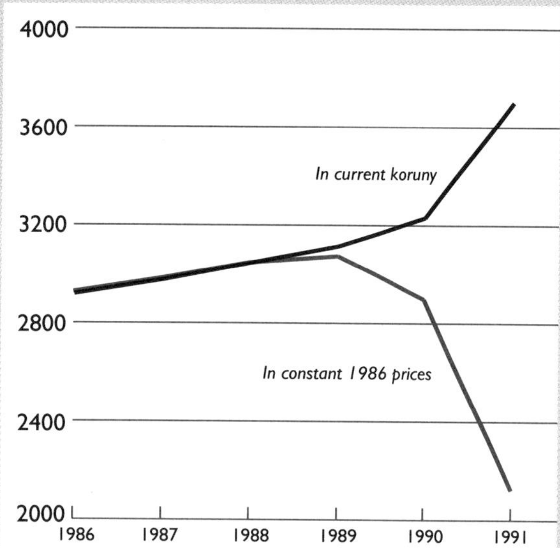

Sources: Czechoslovak authorities; and IMF staff estimates.
[1]Includes wages, bonuses, and other payments.

meaningful valuation of the enterprises, the lack of domestic savings, equity and political considerations, the absence of sophisticated financial instruments and specialists, and the realization that foreign investors would be interested in only the "elite" of the enterprises. Therefore, the idea of free distribution of equity to the public through a "voucher scheme" was elaborated as a necessary method in terms of speed and comprehensiveness, and a desirable one on grounds of equity and political acceptability.

The voucher scheme is a plan to transfer the ownership of a major portion of the large enterprises of Czechoslovakia to the public in general. Every Czechoslovak citizen over the age of 18 will be entitled to acquire a voucher book that will endow him or her with 1,000 investment points. These points can be used to bid for shares of the enterprises being offered or, alternatively, can be tendered in exchange for shares in mutual funds. The mutual funds ("investment privatization funds," or IPFs) can be established with few requirements beyond a minimum capital and a charter. The IPFs must make their investment objectives publicly known, in order to facilitate the decisions of individuals on the use of their vouchers. The IPFs will permit individuals to avoid getting involved in financial analysis of enterprises and to increase their possibilities for a convenient portfolio diversification.

Three successive "waves" of voucher privatization are envisaged, with the first one beginning in early 1992. A potential 11½ million individuals will be able to purchase and register a voucher book at a cost of Kcs 1,000 (about $33, or a week's average wages). In a preliminary round, individuals will have the opportunity to pledge their vouchers to one or several IPFs. (The smallest denomination of vouchers is 100 investment points, so that an individual could opt for 10 different investments.) Next, the first of as many as five rounds of bidding for shares of enterprises will start, with enterprises being offered prices proportional to their book values. The system will not be a full-fledged auction in the sense of reaching market-clearing prices in the vouchers-for-shares exchange. For example, some trades will be concluded in the first rounds while further price changes will take place in later rounds. Thus, part of the equity of some enterprises may be sold at the price offered in the current round, while the remaining shares are offered again at an adjusted (lower) price in later rounds. Also, individual bids will be given some preference over IPFs' bids in order to simplify the process: thus, it is expected that as soon as individuals' demands are satisfied, it will be possible to auction the remaining enterprises among a few IPFs in a less complicated way. The final round will follow some—as yet undecided—mechanism either to allocate all remaining investment points or to determine what value, if any, unused investment points retain.

The basic structure of the voucher privatization scheme is probably the only one that can achieve privatization on such a major scale in a short period of time. Moreover, the scheme has clear political advantages in that it spreads private property widely and avoids favoring the old privileged classes. There are, however, some unavoidable trade-offs between these advantages and some of the shortcomings of the voucher scheme.

A central problem is related to the effectiveness of corporate governance under very diffuse ownership (spanning millions of small shareholders). Enterprise managers would be subject to little effective supervision by owners, with the result that the control of the enterprises would have changed little after privatization. Effective corporate governance requires the presence of at least one large shareholder. Two basic approaches to this problem have been proposed: a complete hands-off attitude, in the expectation that large active shareholders will spontaneously appear in the context of extensive profit opportunities for "corporate raiders,"[17] and

[17]See, for example, Hinds (1991).

an active involvement for the state in designing and organizing financial intermediaries to exercise management supervision on behalf of the public.[18] The Czechoslovak scheme lies somewhere in between these two polar approaches in the sense that, although the state does not take any initiative in designing structures of corporate governance, the creation of financial intermediaries, in the form of IPFs, is encouraged.[19]

There are some doubts, however, as to whether the IPFs will fulfill the role of active supervisors of management. In some cases, the IPFs may in fact serve as vehicles for management/worker buyouts, with employees of an enterprise creating an IPF for the purpose of acquiring stock in their company. But in the rest of the cases, IPFs may limit themselves to providing the possibility of portfolio diversification and other financial services to individuals; while not legally prevented from becoming active shareholders, the IPFs may not naturally tend to assume that role, because that may not be their normal line of business and they may not find it a particularly profitable activity. In addition, there is no mechanism to guarantee the creation of large shareholders, for example by selling shares in large blocks to IPFs.[20]

Aside from problems relating to corporate governance, voucher privatization is subject to various other complications. There may be serious difficulties in achieving "convergence" in a small number of iterations in the process of allocating shares to voucher investment points, and very inequitable situations may arise if the initial prices must be changed substantially in later rounds. Moreover, shares in many of the privatized companies may turn out to be a very illiquid investment for individuals, since it is unlikely that the stock market will comprise a very large number of actively traded stocks.

But perhaps the largest obstacle to a successful privatization is the debt overhang of enterprises, discussed above. Since the financial sector has not operated under market conditions, it is quite possible that some enterprises have negative net worth, which will make their privatization impossible even if they are given away. Even ignoring such extreme cases, highly leveraged positions may cause a large number of failures among the newly privatized enterprises under the prevailing conditions of large structural changes and contraction in aggregate demand.

Not all large enterprises will be privatized through the voucher method. The Government attaches importance to attracting foreign investment and the attendant capital, expertise, technology, and access to markets; at a minimum, those enterprises for which there is definite foreign investor interest (expressed in specific offers) are likely to be excluded from voucher privatization. Still, the scale of voucher privatization will be massive: it might involve some three fourths of the total of approximately 2,500 large enterprises in the first wave. Some further 10 percent to 15 percent are expected to be privatized through direct, standard methods mostly to foreign investors or, in some cases, to managers and workers. The remaining enterprises will require liquidation or, perhaps, restructuring; to facilitate the liquidation process, a bankruptcy law was adopted in July 1991.

As is the case for small enterprises, the laws on restitution of property provide for restitution or compensation for ownership of larger enterprises expropriated after 1948. In order to spare the privatization process from further complications, strict time limits have been set for both applications for restitution and the resolution of claims, and the law has granted the state the option to compensate the claimant in cash (or in equity shares) rather than with the actual property. Enterprises against which restitution claims are pending will not be entered into the privatization process. Any further liabilities that might arise as a result of the restitution process will be liabilities of the state, rather than of the new owners of an enterprise.

Despite the substantial difficulties still remaining, considering both its scale and its advanced stage of preparation, the privatization effort in Czechoslovakia appears to be one of the most advanced in Central and Eastern Europe. While Poland and Romania have passed legislation to support voucher-type mass privatization, they are far behind Czechoslovakia in implementation.[21] Hungary has embarked on a slower process of selling off enterprises on a case-by-case basis, while Bulgaria has yet to decide which method to adopt. The former German Democratic Republic has privatized a substantial fraction of industrial enterprises, but this process is becoming far lengthier and more difficult than had been expected, despite the favorable conditions associated with its integration in the Federal Republic of Germany (and the European Community).

---

[18]See, for example, Lipton and Sachs (1990).

[19]The trade-offs involved in different mass privatization schemes are discussed in Borensztein (1991).

[20]Moreover, with a view to furthering the risk-spreading role of the IPFs, the authorities are considering regulations that would limit their ability to acquire a very large interest in any given company or to concentrate their interests in only one or a very few companies.

[21]See Demekas and Khan (1991).

IV Economic Developments During the Stabilization Phase

The reform program was expected to have a considerable impact on the evolution of prices, output, and the balance of payments, through both the effects of the macroeconomic stabilization process and the transformation of the productive structure demanded by the creation of a market economy. Developments on the price and balance of payments fronts have been very encouraging, indicating that the reform program is progressing solidly. Although the decline in output was larger than anticipated, it is partly explained by the fall in demand for Czechoslovak exports from the members of the former CMEA.

Price Developments

Price developments following the big bang fell into two well-defined stages: the initial price "jump" in the first few weeks after price liberalization and the subsequent stabilization stage. The magnitude of the price jump widely exceeded the (optimistic) working assumption utilized in the formulation of policies. The price jump, as argued below, reflected primarily supply factors and had little to do with the stance of aggregate demand policies. The first surge in prices worked itself out in the first two months of the year and, after March, inflation was rapidly brought under control. This harnessing of inflation is perhaps the greatest success of the stabilization efforts that were part of the radical reform program of 1991.

The initial price jump came as no surprise. The collapse of the CMEA and such policy actions as the change in the exchange rate, changes in administered prices, and the removal of subsidies on certain goods had been expected to generate a large rise in the price level. In addition, there was likely to be a direct effect of price liberalization, as relative prices shifted in favor of goods previously in short supply.

At a macroeconomic level, the size of such a price jump is also related to the extent of "monetary overhang," or the monetary disequilibrium existing at the controlled price level. Although the precise concept—and even more so the measurement—of monetary overhang is elusive, a desire of the population to reduce its holdings of money can stimulate an increased demand for goods and thus amplify the price jump. However, the adjustment of prices to the disequilibrium in the money market is probably a much slower process than the price response to direct measures, such as a devaluation of the exchange rate or the removal of subsidies. Moreover, indications in Czechoslovakia were that, owing to prudent policies in the past, any monetary overhang was small, and a sharp fall in retail sales as early as January (by over one fourth in real terms, compared with a year earlier) suggests that this assessment was correct.

During January–February, at the producer and retail level, prices jumped on average by about 45 percent. This increase was relatively small when compared with the increases in other previously centrally planned economies that had recently undergone price liberalization, especially considering that liberalization in Czechoslovakia coincided with the move to world prices in CMEA trade. This indicates that the shortages and monetary disequilibrium in Czechoslovakia were less severe, and that the need for an adjustment in relative prices, such as the exchange rate, was smaller.

Prices continued to increase after February, but at a rapidly decelerating pace. The prices of some of the important energy products were increased in May. Moreover, the initial price increases set off a chain reaction of cost increases in other sectors that took some time to work their way through the economy; this process included the partial indexation of wages permitted under the Government's agreement with enterprises and trade unions. These secondary waves of price increases explain a good portion of the inflation in months after the price jump, but prices rapidly stabilized nevertheless (Chart 7). Between March and June, producer prices increased by 4 percent and consumer prices by 11 percent; in the four months from June to October, industrial producer prices fell by 0.5 percent and consumer prices rose by only 0.2 percent. The higher persistence of inflation at the consumer level is in part explained by a slower adjustment of

Chart 7. Evolution of Prices

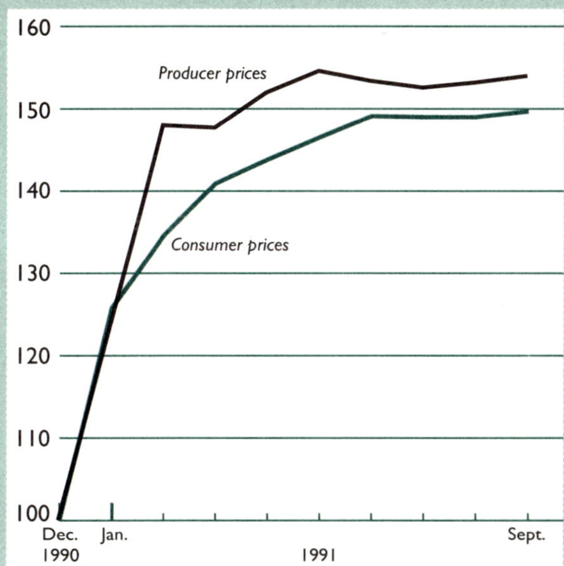

Source: Czechoslovak authorities.

prices at the retail level, as the initial increase was also more moderate in consumer prices than in producer prices.

Output Developments

In Czechoslovakia, as in all the other formerly centrally planned economies, output fell sharply following the structural reforms. In the first half of 1991, industrial output fell by 17 percent, construction activity by 26 percent, and the volume of retail sales by almost 30 percent, compared with the same period in 1990. For 1991, the fall in GDP may reach 12–15 percent. These figures may exaggerate the actual decline in output and sales owing to underrecording of private sector activity and, in the case of retail sales, of personal imports. In addition, output figures must be interpreted with caution, given the questionable value of some of the output produced under central planning. However, it is unlikely that the overall picture would change materially if it were possible to correct fully for these factors.

The contraction in output in state enterprises also caused a steady increase in unemployment from the beginning of 1991, with the rate of unemployment reaching 6 percent in October. Layoffs accounted for 90 percent of the approximately fifty thousand workers who became unemployed every month. Reflecting important structural changes in production, the regional disparities are sharp and increasing (Chart 8). In the region of Prague, for example, the unemployment rate was below 1.5 percent in October, while in most parts of Slovakia, where much of the industrial base is becoming obsolete with the changes in the pattern of international trade, unemployment already exceeded 10 percent.

The decline in output was associated with a number of factors—some of them quite independent of the reform process—the relative magnitude of which is not easy to assess. The paper examines in turn the external shock associated with developments in the CMEA, the changes in structure of production, the combination of the price jump and restrictive policies, and the fall in domestic demand owing to uncertainty.

External Shock

The Czechoslovak economy suffered a double external shock from developments in the CMEA area. First, exports to the former CMEA area fell precipitously as the economic crisis in the former U.S.S.R. worsened and other Eastern European economies faced difficult adjustment processes. Moreover, as CMEA trade moved to a convertible currency basis, some of Czechoslovakia's competitive edge was blunted and difficulties were experienced in trading under the new system. Despite some recovery after the first quarter of the year, the volume of exports to the former CMEA is estimated to have fallen by about two thirds for the year as a whole, and could account for a decline in output of 8 percent. Second, the switch to international pricing in CMEA trade meant a terms of trade deterioration for Czechoslovakia: the severalfold increase in prices of energy and other imported industrial inputs could, by itself, account for a significant contraction in output, especially in energy-intensive sectors.

Changes in Structure of Production

Starting from a widely distorted position, the move to a market system together with the lifting of barriers to international trade necessarily implies large changes in the structure of production. Consumers, free from the "forced substitution" regime that made them buy whatever was available, will turn away from noncompetitive products in favor of imports or more acceptable domestic substitutes. It should thus be expected that many enterprises—and some entire production branches—would decline and perhaps not survive under the new system. This effect, per se, does not imply a fall in output, but only a change in its composition.

Chart 8. Unemployment Rate[1]

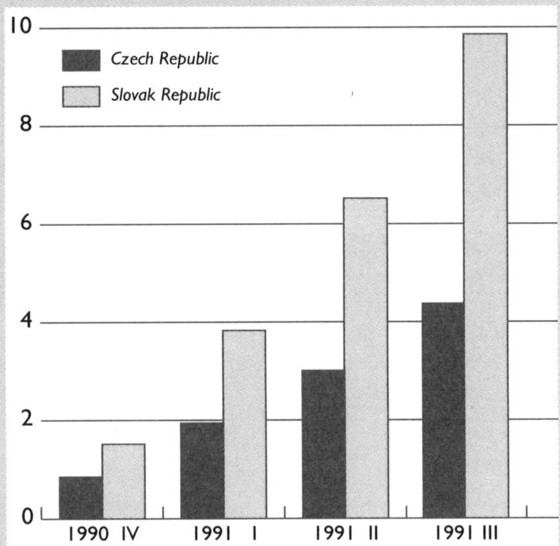

Source: Czechoslovak authorities.
[1]End of period.

An asymmetric speed of adjustment is to be expected, however, in the reallocation of production, because an expansion in the productive capacity of an enterprise requires time for planning, investment and recruitment, building of structures, and so forth, while a reduction or interruption of production can be effected almost immediately, especially under financial distress. Furthermore, the privatization prospects and uncertainties about the new environment may discourage enterprises from undertaking any long-term commitments to increase or restructure productive capacity, making their response even more sluggish.

Restrictive Policies After the Price Jump

Although a sudden price increase in the first weeks of 1991 was unavoidable, a tight and nonaccommodating stance for financial policies was thought to be essential to avoid the emergence of an inflationary process. In these conditions, it has been suggested[22] that tight credit conditions, in conjunction with increased costs of raw materials and other inputs, would generate an aggregate supply contraction. The actual price jump was much higher than assumed when the (deliberately conservative) targets for fiscal and monetary aggregates were established, and financial policies were adjusted with some delay to accommodate the higher price jump. Moreover, for a number of reasons explained above, the policy stance was even tighter than planned, particularly in the first quarter.

Fall in Domestic Demand

Several factors combined to weaken demand by consumers and enterprises over and above the effect of tight financial and incomes policies.[23] In large measure these factors derived from the uncertainty generated by the transition to a market economy. From the point of view of enterprises, large investment plans were almost precluded in the transition phase because of uncertainty and the expectation of privatization. Uncertainty about future rules and regulations concerning a broad spectrum of legal, tax, and environmental issues, and even about the structure of relative prices, makes it difficult to evaluate any investment project. Insofar as the prospective privatization would be likely to entail changes in corporate strategy, the logical decision by management would be that any large commitment of funds should wait for approval by the new ownership.

From the point of view of consumers, uncertainty about the evolution of the real wage and poor job security must have dampened what had been feared would be a spending burst after years of repressed consumption of domestic and imported goods. In addition—although reliable data on inventories are not available—the demand for (voluntary) inventory accumulation must have fallen sharply as the move to market rules eliminated the main motive for enterprises to keep large holdings of inventories, namely, the uncertain availability of inputs, while changes in financial markets curtailed the favorable financing that inventory holding had received in the past. The buildup of inventories that took place in the last few months of 1990, in anticipation of devaluation and price increases, probably accentuated the depletion of input inventories in 1991. On the other hand, as sales fell short of production, there is thought to have been an involuntary accumulation of output inventories, probably presaging a further fall in output.

Relative Importance of Supply and Demand Factors

An examination of the evolution of the different branches in the industrial sector may shed some

[22]See Calvo and Coricelli (1992).

[23]See Blanchard and others (1991) on aggregate demand behavior in the transition phase.

Table 4. Output and Price Changes in the Industrial Sector

Industrial Sector	Change in Output[1]	Change in Relative Price[2]	Change in Relative Price[3]
Fuel	2.4	–26.2	–4.7
Energy	–1.7	4.8	39.6
Iron metallurgy	–7.7	20.9	4.8
Nonferrous metallurgy	–30.8	33.0	14.9
Chemical and rubber	–18.9	–14.8	27.9
Machinery	–18.7	11.9	–2.6
Electronics	–28.4	12.5	–2.1
Building materials	–26.9	12.5	–2.7
Woodwork	–12.4	11.2	–3.8
Metalwork	–19.5	31.3	14.3
Paper and cellulose	–4.9	24.2	7.0
Glass, ceramics, and porcelain	–19.0	26.0	9.3
Textiles	–25.0	17.9	1.7
Clothing	–36.7	–0.4	–14.0
Tanning	–26.0	20.0	3.7
Printing	–19.5	39.4	20.3
Food	–21.6	–20.6	–31.5
Frozen foods, spring water, and tobacco	–19.8	51.0	30.5
Others	—	7.1	–7.4
Total industry	–17.6	—	—

Sources: Czechoslovak authorities; and IMF staff estimates.
[1]January–June 1991 relative to January–June 1990 (in percent).
[2]Relative price increase from January to June 1991 (in percent).
[3]Relative price increase from July 1990 to June 1991 (in percent).

light on the relative importance of the different determinants of the drop in output (Table 4). The data display the change in production level in the first half of 1991 relative to the same period in 1990. Although the output contraction is fairly generalized, the sharpest fall took place in sectors that are believed to include some of the products with the least comparative advantage, such as clothing and electronics.[24] Another of the largest drops was in construction materials, reflecting the low level of investment in structures. That all sectors, with the exception of fuels, experienced a decline in output, however, does suggest that macroeconomic forces also played a role. There is no clear correlation between output and relative price changes—either negative, which would suggest a leading role for supply-side factors, nor positive, which would suggest a predominance of demand-side factors.

[24]As the sectors thought to have the least comparative advantage are also often those that exported significantly to the rest of the CMEA, it is of course difficult to discern the relative importance of the opening to competition and the loss of CMEA markets.

Balance of Payments Developments

Several opposing influences combined to produce, in the aggregate, a better-than-expected balance of payments result during the first half of the year (Table 5). A very weak demand for exports by countries in the former CMEA area generated a drop in export receipts, while exports to other areas were also somewhat disappointing—especially in the first quarter. The fall in exports, however, was more than offset by a very steep drop in imports (Chart 9). The capital account suffered from delays in expected disbursements of official balance of payments support, but foreign investment inflows were substantial—albeit driven mainly by a single large transaction.

The drop in exports to the CMEA countries, although larger than projected, was to be expected. However, the sluggish expansion of exports to market economies, particularly in the first quarter of the year, was something of a puzzle especially in light of the gain in competitiveness associated with the exchange rate depreciation and the policy of

Table 5. Balance of Payments
(In billions of U.S. dollars)

	1990 Revised			First Half 1991		
	Non-CMEA[1]	CMEA & Clearing	Total	Convertible currency	Clearing	Total
Current account	–0.9	–0.3	–1.2	–0.4	0.3	—
Trade balance	–0.7	–0.8	–1.4	–0.5	0.2	–0.3
Exports, f.o.b.	5.9	5.8	11.6	3.6	1.2	4.7
Imports, c.i.f.	–6.5	–6.5	–13.1	–4.1	–0.9	–5.0
Of which: oil and gas[2]	(–0.2)	(–2.9)	(–3.1)	(–1.0)	(–0.6)	(–1.6)
Services balance	—	0.2	0.2	0.3	0.1	0.4
Receipts	1.7	1.0	2.7	1.0	0.2	1.2
Payments	–1.6	–0.8	–2.4	–0.8	–0.1	–0.9
Income balance	–0.3	0.1	–0.3	–0.1	—	–0.1
Receipts	0.4	0.1	0.5	0.1	—	0.1
Payments	–0.7	—	–0.8	–0.2	—	–0.2
Transfers (net)	—	0.2	0.2	—	—	—
Capital account	0.1	0.4	0.5	—	–0.5	–0.5
Direct investment (net)	0.2	—	0.2	0.4	—	0.4
Suppliers' credits	–0.1	0.4	0.3	–0.4	–0.5	–0.9
Net medium-/long-term credit extended	—	–0.2	–0.2	0.3	–0.2	0.1
Net medium-/long-term credit received	0.3	—	0.3	–0.3	—	–0.3
Short-term (net)	–0.3	0.6	0.2	–0.3	–0.3	–0.6
Valuation changes, errors, and omissions	–0.6	–0.1	–0.7	0.3	0.2	0.5
Overall balance	–1.4	—	–1.4	—	—	—
Financing	. . .	. . .	1.4	. . .	. . .	—
Use of gross reserves	. . .	. . .	1.1	. . .	. . .	–0.5
Use of IMF credit	. . .	. . .	. . .	. . .	. . .	1.0
Other official support	. . .	. . .	. . .	. . .	. . .	—
Other bank liabilities	. . .	. . .	0.3	. . .	. . .	–0.5
Short-term liabilities	. . .	. . .	–0.3	. . .	. . .	–0.3
Market borrowing	. . .	. . .	0.5	. . .	. . .	—
Net other (including valuation changes)	. . .	. . .	0.1	. . .	. . .	–0.2
Memorandum items:						
Total balance of payments support	. . .	. . .	. . .	. . .	. . .	1.0
Gross reserves at end of period	. . .	. . .	1.2	. . .	. . .	1.7
(In months of following-year imports)	. . .	. . .	(1.4)	. . .	. . .	. . .
Net reserves at end of period	. . .	. . .	–2.6	. . .	. . .	–2.6

Sources: Czechoslovak authorities; and IMF staff estimates.
[1]Data were converted from transferable rubles to U.S. dollars at cross rates and therefore are not comparable to data for 1991.
[2]Indicative only; data are on a trade basis and are not strictly consistent with the overall import figures shown.

Chart 9. Export and Import Volumes

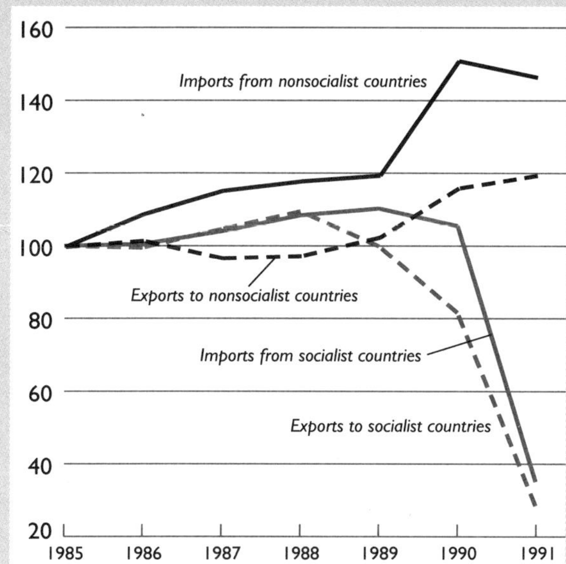

Sources: Czechoslovak authorities; and IMF staff estimates.

Chart 11. Export and Import Unit Values

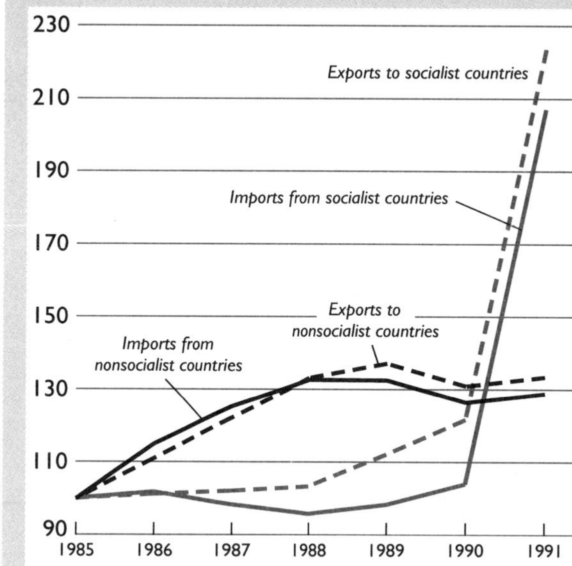

Sources: Czechoslovak authorities; and IMF staff estimates.

wage restraint (Chart 10). Clearly, the particular structure of the export sector of Czechoslovakia was not conducive to a rapid increase in exports to Western markets.[25] Also, several other factors worked to offset some of the effect of improved competitiveness: the policy-induced reduction in exports of armaments; the increase in the cost of key raw materials imported from the former CMEA (Chart 11); the loss of economies of scale as demand from the former CMEA area and from domestic sources fell sharply; and the disruption of previous trading links as enterprises specializing in foreign trade were restructured.

Chart 10. Effective Exchange Rates

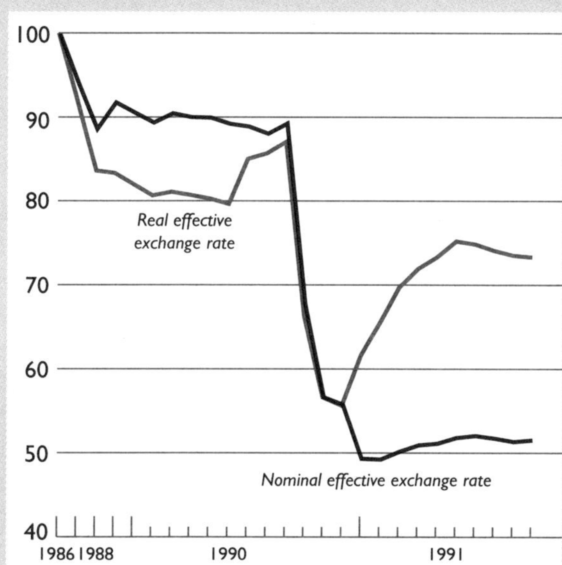

Source: IMF staff estimates.

The low level of non-oil imports is obviously linked to the weakness of domestic demand, both for investment and consumption purposes. Imports may also have been dampened by a slow response of the import sector to bring onto the domestic market imported consumer goods that enjoy a competitive advantage over their local substitutes. An additional factor might have been the imposition of the temporary import surcharge on consumer goods. Although at its original level of 20 percent the surcharge might appear to be only a moderate influence, the fact that it was known to be temporary might have encouraged potential importers to postpone their purchase plans. Despite this relatively sluggish performance of trade with

[25]Prominent among Czechoslovakia's exports are armaments, heavy machinery with a slow marketing process, and manufactures that may not be competitive outside the CMEA area; also potentially important are agricultural, steel, and textile products that face various trade barriers in Western Europe in particular.

Chart 12. Direction of Trade: Exports
(In percent)

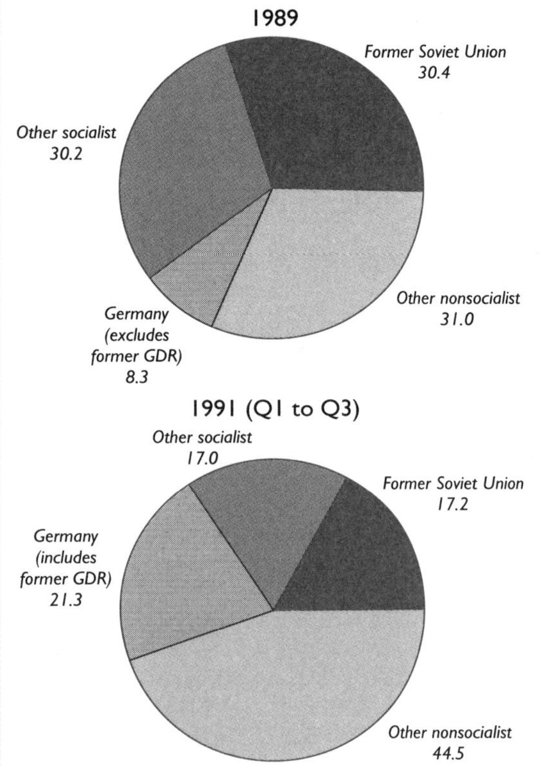

Sources: Czechoslovak authorities; and IMF staff estimates.

Chart 13. Direction of Trade: Imports
(In percent)

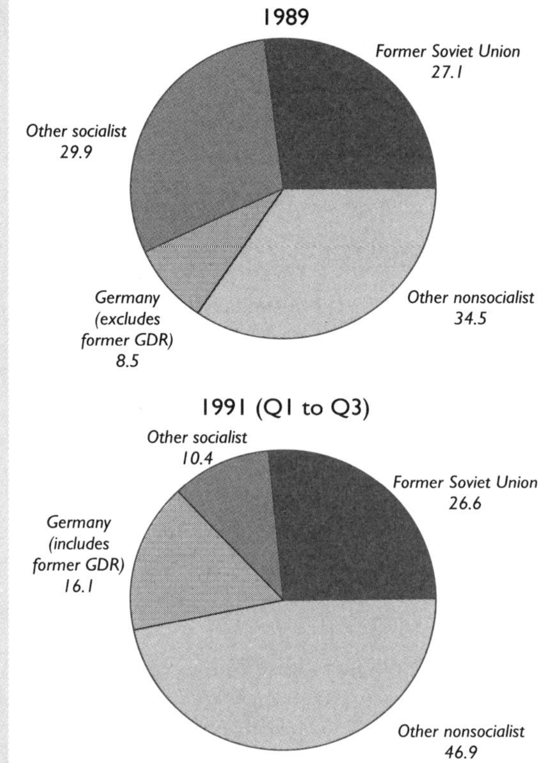

Sources: Czechoslovak authorities; and IMF staff estimates.

market economies, in 1991 the geographical composition of the international trade of Czechoslovakia shifted quickly toward Western countries (Charts 12 and 13).

Tight financial policies and adequate interest rates—including a moderate premium over those prevailing in international capital markets—helped prevent major pressures on international reserves; the lack of large-scale speculative outflows was also reflected in the fact that the premium in parallel foreign exchange markets never reached significant levels after January 1.

V Lessons Learned and the Task Ahead

The example of Czechoslovakia's early stabilization success has shown that a previously centrally planned economy with limited macroeconomic imbalances can weather the cumulated effects of a large-scale liberalization and a severe terms of trade shock without letting either inflation or the external imbalance get out of hand. In Czechoslovakia's case, the key to this success was a combination of restrictive fiscal, monetary, and incomes policies, as well as a realistic and stable exchange rate. Exchange rate policy had been the subject of particularly intense debate, but events seem to confirm that the exchange rate anchor provided a reference point around which newly freed prices arranged themselves quickly. Interestingly, and in contrast to some of its neighbors, Czechoslovakia allowed ex post real interest rates to be negative during the period of the price jump. This policy does not seem to have interfered with the stabilization effort at all, suggesting that, abstracting away from the initial price jump, inflationary expectations may have indeed been quite low.

At the same time, the decline in economic activity has been large. It is impossible to say quite how much of Czechoslovakia's productive structure has become uneconomic, following the dismantling of the special trade arrangements of the former CMEA and the opening of the economy to the rest of the world. What is clear is that the new activities, which must eventually offset the termination of old ones, are emerging slowly. At the same time, however, it is possible that the decline in output has not been large enough. Many enterprises appear to be continuing to produce, for inventory or at a loss, while financing themselves by any means possible—notably by accumulating large debts to their suppliers. There are also other worrisome signs that enterprises may begin to clamor more loudly for the relief from government—in the form of subsidies, guarantees, and subsidized credits—that has hitherto been denied them. The Government will need to stand firm in resisting these demands and seek the rapid termination of loss-making production to avoid crowding out new initiatives and to avert the danger of a financial gridlock in the enterprise sector.

In large part, these developments may be a characteristic of the no-man's-land in which central planning has already been abandoned, but a market system is still far from established. Ahead of both large-scale privatization and action to deal with enterprises' inherited debt burden, plans to invest or to change the structure of production await decisions of new owners, and banks cannot properly evaluate projects. Although no Central or Eastern European country can yet offer any lessons on methods of privatization, the Czechoslovak example does demonstrate the perils of remaining in such a no-man's-land and the need for the greatest possible speed in structural reform.

The success of Czechoslovakia's initial stabilization effort thus marks only the first step in a long process of transformation. It is essential now that the hard-earned success of stabilization be safeguarded through the coming period, which is likely to become even more difficult on the fiscal front. But internal and external balances are only a necessary, and by no means sufficient, condition for growth, and the uncharted path of creating a dynamic market economy out of the remnants of the old system still lies ahead. As was the case with its introduction, the dismantling of central planning is happening for the first time in history. The ultimate objective of the transformation is clear, and a great deal is known about the framework, institutions, and policies that shape market economies. There is, however, no blueprint for getting from here to there.

Some crucial steps have already been taken in the process of structural reform. On January 1, 1991, those elements of reform that could be instituted at the stroke of a pen—devaluation and large-scale price and trade liberalization—were implemented, putting in place the main signals necessary for the workings of a market system. There now remains, however, the much more complex work of ensuring the effective transmission of these signals through the economy, and ensuring that appropriate incentives are in place to make economic agents react in an efficient manner. Four tasks stand out in this regard.

First, the Government will have to provide the entire framework of a market economy. A large part of the necessary legal system has already been put in place. However, the building of institutions to administer this system (such as antitrust and bank supervision offices) and to fulfill the other supportive functions of government (such as labor exchanges or trade and investment promotion activities) will inevitably take time, as will the provision of modern basic infrastructure.

Second, government interference with market signals should be minimized—the Government will need to refine the rather blunt instruments with which it has thus far conducted macroeconomic policy. To this end, a number of plans are under way, including a major tax reform in 1993, which should "level the playing field" and permit a more even spreading of the tax burden through a widening of the tax base; a replacement of the clearly distortionary direct credit ceilings on banks with instruments of reserve money management; and a phasing out of the excess wage tax.

Third, "noise" from the past should not be allowed to contaminate signals in the present. In this respect, it is particularly worrisome that the burden of bank debt inherited by enterprises from the old system obscures their current viability. Various solutions to this problem have been proposed, ranging from a complete write-off of debts as of some cut-off date to case-by-case debt workouts. A full solution is urgent; in October 1991, the Czechoslovak Government announced an important step in this direction in the form of a plan to write off a certain amount of enterprise debts ahead of privatization.

Finally, ensuring a "clean" transmission of signals through the system is not sufficient to ensure an efficient allocation of resources: economic agents need also to react to these signals in an efficient manner. Thus, more than all other structural measures, privatization is the key to the success of the reform effort. As outlined above, the absence of well-established markets implies that conventional methods would not achieve privatization on any major scale within the time frame desired. The Government's chosen strategy is an eclectic mix of methods, which seeks a balance between the sometimes conflicting objectives of speed, of attracting appropriate expertise and capital, of raising public resources, and of political expediency. It cannot be overemphasized that little improvement in economic performance can be expected ahead of privatization, and hence that all efforts should be made to accelerate the process.

The structural measures required to lay the basis for a thriving market economy will take time. Moreover, there will be lags between implementation of these measures, decisions by economic agents to react to them, implementation of these decisions, and, finally, results. The nearly complete absence of an entrepreneurial tradition will lengthen this process significantly. It is impossible at this stage to predict just how long all these lags will delay an improvement in economic performance, particularly in the context of a highly uncertain, and perhaps worsening, regional economic climate. The challenge facing the Czechoslovak authorities now is to persevere with reform without losing the support of the public. This task will require political leadership capable of explaining the process and of containing the aspirations and impatience of the population. However, the maintenance of a relatively firm political and social consensus on reform through the turbulent early phase of reform has raised the odds in favor of success.

Statistical Appendix

Table A1. Revenue of General Government[1]

(In billions of koruny)

	1986	1987	1988	1989	1990	Revised Budget 1991
Federation and republics						
Total revenue	323.8	345.3	359.3	374.3	390.3	482.5
Tax revenue	293.7	313.7	327.8	326.4	368.2	464.3
Income and profits taxes	148.7	160.0	158.1	78.4	93.7	192.9
Population	32.5	33.6	34.7	0.2	0.3	56.1
Wages tax	32.4	33.4	34.5	—	—	55.9
Literary/artists tax	0.1	0.2	0.2	0.2	0.3	0.2
Profits taxes	116.2	126.4	123.6	78.2	93.4	136.8
Enterprises	97.6	107.0	104.4	67.9	84.1	. . .
Financial companies	18.6	19.3	19.0	8.8	6.8	. . .
Agricultural profit tax	—	—	—	1.5	2.5	. . .
Payroll tax	29.3	32.9	37.0	95.4	98.4	117.8
Domestic taxes on goods and services	110.7	110.9	116.7	134.6	147.8	141.9
Turnover tax (gross)	103.0	104.0	108.3	124.8	147.8	141.9
Internal market differential	7.7	6.9	8.4	9.8	—	—
Taxes on international trade	5.0	10.0	15.9	13.9	25.8	8.8
Customs duties[2]	0.2	0.2	0.3	0.5	6.5	8.8
Other foreign trade levies	4.8	9.8	15.6	13.4	19.3	—
Other taxes	—	—	—	4.1	2.5	2.9
Nontax revenue	33.7	30.1	32.1	44.6	31.0	18.2
Entrepreneurial and property income	25.2	21.6	23.0	29.7	16.9	14.3
Transfers from subsidiary organizations	0.2	0.1	0.2	0.2	0.2	0.4
Other	25.0	21.5	22.9	29.5	16.7	13.9
Administrative fees	1.2	1.2	1.4	8.3	9.1	1.7
Fines and forfeits	0.3	0.4	0.4	0.4	0.1	. . .
Other nontax revenue	7.0	7.0	7.3	6.2	4.9	2.2
Capital revenue	—	—	—	—	—	—
Timing adjustment	–3.5	1.5	–0.6	3.3	–8.9	—
Local authorities						
Total revenue	128.2	134.0	141.1	151.9	162.4	95.6
Tax revenue	44.2	45.2	47.7	76.6	81.3	11.4
Income and profits taxes	25.6	26.3	27.9	57.3	61.3	5.9
Wages tax	15.2	15.9	16.6	52.3	54.4	3.0
Corporate taxes	10.4	10.4	11.3	5.0	6.9	2.9
Payroll tax[3]	11.4	11.7	2.2	—	—	5.5
Domestic taxes on goods and services	7.1	7.2	7.6	—	—	—
Other taxes[3]	—	—	—	19.3	20.0	—
Nontax revenue	15.9	18.2	19.2	17.1	17.3	6.1
Entrepreneurial and property income	11.5	12.1	12.3	1.0	1.0	—
Fees and fines	0.5	0.6	0.6	6.8	7.3	1.1
Other nontax revenue	3.9	5.5	6.2	9.3	9.0	5.0
Capital revenue	0.2	0.2	0.2	0.1	0.2	—
Transfers from other government	68.0	70.4	74.1	58.1	63.6	78.1
Extrabudgetary funds						
Total revenue	4.6	4.5	4.3	5.5	4.0	3.6
Nontax revenue	3.1	3.0	2.9	4.0	3.7	2.7
Transfers (from other government)	1.4	1.5	1.4	1.5	0.3	0.9
Memorandum items:						
Net turnover tax[4]	82.1	81.1	86.9	85.5	113.2	141.9
Net foreign trade surrenders[5]	–12.8	–8.1	–3.0	–13.7	—	—
Total revenue (percent of GDP)	55.7	57.9	58.0	62.1	60.2	47.4

Source: Czechoslovak authorities.
[1]Data from 1989 onward are consistent with methodology of *Government Finance Statistics*; data through 1988 are not. General government includes operations under state budgets and state financial assets and liabilities and excludes operations of subsidized organizations and funds of the ministries.
[2]Includes import surcharge in 1991.
[3]Some payroll tax at local authority level is classified as other taxes in 1989–90.
[4]Turnover tax net of negative turnover tax (shown under expenditure). Includes internal market differential.
[5]Foreign trade levies net of foreign trade subsidies (shown under expenditure).

Table A2. Expenditure of General Government by Economic Category[1]
(In billions of koruny)

	1986	1987	1988	1989	1990	Revised Budget 1991[2]
Federation and republics						
Total expenditure	339.9	347.4	384.2	401.0	442.9	474.5
Current expenditure	288.0	301.7	332.5	349.1	389.0	431.7
Consumption	78.2	86.1	90.7	80.5	83.5	132.8
Wages and salaries	17.8	18.4	19.1	17.6	17.5	28.5
Services	60.4	67.7	71.6	62.9	66.0	105.7
Interest	—	—	—	0.2	1.7	2.8
Current transfers	209.8	215.6	241.8	268.4	303.8	296.2
Transfers to households	83.0	84.2	86.6	100.0	108.3	159.9
Unemployment benefits	—	—	—	—	—	9.8
Universal income support	—	—	—	—	12.7	32.0
Pensions	54.2	55.6	57.6	61.6	63.6	. . .
Sick pay	8.9	8.7	8.9	9.6	10.0	. . .
Family benefits	16.4	16.3	16.2	16.5	18.9	. . .
Other	3.5	3.6	3.9	12.3	3.1	. . .
To local authorities	43.1	45.3	47.7	30.2	33.4	63.0
To extrabudgetary funds	1.4	1.5	1.4	1.5	0.3	0.9
To subsidized organizations[3]	2.1	2.1	2.3	2.5	3.2	11.4
To enterprises and agricultural cooperatives	80.3	82.5	103.8	133.5	157.6	60.6
Retail subsidies[4]	28.6	29.8	29.8	49.1	34.6	—
Foreign trade subsidies	17.6	17.9	18.6	27.1	19.3	—
Stock adjustments[5]	—	—	15.5	8.0	54.4	—
Other[4]	34.1	34.8	39.9	49.3	49.3	60.6
Transfers abroad	—	—	—	0.7	1.0	0.4
Capital expenditure and net lending	46.5	48.6	51.2	49.6	53.0	42.8
By budgetary organizations	7.3	7.5	7.8	6.4	7.2	14.3
Capital transfers	35.0	35.2	35.7	37.8	45.1	33.2
To local authorities	24.9	25.2	26.4	27.9	30.2	15.2
To subsidized organizations[3]	. . .	. . .	. . .	. . .	. . .	3.7
To enterprises	10.1	10.1	9.3	9.8	14.8	14.3
Net lending	4.2	5.8	7.7	5.4	0.7	–4.7
Timing adjustment	5.4	–2.8	0.4	2.3	0.9	—
Local authorities						
Total expenditure	130.7	137.0	142.8	151.4	163.3	95.6
Current expenditure	104.1	110.1	114.6	121.4	131.7	73.8
Consumption	79.2	83.2	87.2	92.7	100.9	63.9
Wages, salaries, travel	29.7	30.8	32.1	32.6	35.3	. . .
Other	49.5	52.4	55.1	60.1	65.6	. . .
Current transfers	24.9	26.9	27.4	28.7	30.8	9.9
Social security outlays	4.2	4.3	4.4	. . .	. . .	1.9
To subsidized organizations[3]	2.9	3.0	3.0	3.3	3.4	—
To enterprises and agricultural cooperatives	17.8	19.6	20.0	. . .	. . .	8.0
Capital expenditure and transfers	26.7	26.9	28.2	30.0	31.6	21.8
By budgetary organizations	21.9	22.4	23.3	4.6	7.8	19.6
Capital transfers to enterprises[3]	4.8	4.5	4.9	25.4	23.8	2.2
Extrabudgetary funds						
Total expenditure	4.7	4.7	4.4	5.3	4.2	3.6
Current expenditure	2.3	1.8	1.6	3.8	2.3	1.2
Transfers to enterprises	2.2	1.5	1.6	3.8	2.3	1.2
Other transfers	0.1	0.3	—	—	—	—
Capital expenditure	2.4	2.9	2.8	1.5	1.9	2.4
Memorandum item:						
Total expenditure, excluding stock adjustments (percent of GDP)	58.4	58.7	59.5	64.5	60.1	46.7

Source: Czechoslovak authorities.
[1]Data from 1989 onward are consistent with methodology of *Government Finance Statistics*; data through 1988 are not. General government includes operations under state budgets and state financial assets and liabilities and excludes operations of subsidized organizations and funds of the ministries.
[2]Operations under state budgets only.
[3]Where the breakdown is not available, all transfers to subsidized organizations are classified as current transfers.
[4]Retail subsidies on energy products are included in "other" in 1991.
[5]Includes transfer to cover debts of retail trade organizations (1988) and transfers to the banks to cover devaluation losses (1990).

Table A3. Budgetary Subsidies[1]

(In billions of koruny)

	1986	1987	1988	1989	1990	Revised Budget 1991
Total budgetary subsidies	85.4	88.7	96.1	122.1	105.9	68.6
(percent of GDP)	12.3	12.5	13.0	16.1	12.9	6.5
Subsidies to enterprises and agricultural cooperatives	39.2	41.1	47.7	59.2	61.5	68.6
(percent of GDP)	5.6	5.8	6.4	7.8	7.5	6.5
Agriculture and foodstuffs	23.7	22.5	26.3	35.0	36.7	23.9
Of which:						
Differential charge	12.4	12.5	12.6	15.0	15.9	—
Charge to prices	1.1	0.9	1.9	4.5	9.4	—
Price fund	—	—	—	4.7	3.2	—
Fund for Market Regulation	—	—	—	—	—	8.4
Other	10.3	9.1	11.9	10.8	8.2	15.5
Industry and construction	3.7	4.3	4.8	8.3	7.0	18.1
Of which:						
Mining	1.4	1.4	1.4	1.3	0.9	0.4
Residential heating[2]	1.5	1.6	2.2	2.3	2.4	13.7
Restructuring[3]	—	—	—	—	2.2	3.0
Iraq embargo	—	—	—	—	—	1.0
Other subsidies to enterprises	11.7	14.3	16.6	15.9	17.8	26.6
Of which:						
Housing	6.1	6.4	6.3	5.0	5.3	10.0
Rents	6.1	6.4	6.3	5.0	. . .	2.9
Low-interest loans	—	—	—	—	. . .	7.1
Urban transport	3.6	4.0	4.3	4.8	4.2	4.3
Railway	. . .	. . .	. . .	. . .	1.3	2.8
Road transport	. . .	. . .	. . .	. . .	2.9	4.8
Forestry and water	—	1.3	1.4	4.9	1.8	. . .
Acid rain (forests)	0.4	0.5	0.7	. . .	. . .	1.5
Retail subsidies	28.6	29.8	29.8	49.1	34.6	. . .
(percent of GDP)	4.1	4.2	4.0	6.5	4.2	—
Foodstuffs	18.7	19.4	19.4	36.1	20.2	—
Of which:						
Dairy	9.1	9.6	9.4	13.0	7.0	—
Meat and meat products	4.4	4.5	4.5	11.9	6.4	—
Fruit and vegetables	2.1	2.1	2.2	2.6	1.5	—
Milling and bakery	0.9	0.9	0.9	3.0	1.6	—
Nonalcoholic drinks	0.3	0.2	0.2	0.3	0.2	—
Nonfood consumer subsidies	9.9	10.3	10.4	12.9	14.4	—
Of which:						
Coal[2]	3.9	4.0	4.2	5.1	5.6	. . .
Gas[2]	2.9	3.3	3.3	2.0	2.2	. . .
Newspapers and printed matter	0.3	0.3	0.3	0.7	—	—
Brick materials (construction)	0.3	0.4	0.4	0.8	1.6	—
Foreign trade subsidies	17.6	17.9	18.6	13.9	9.8	—
(percent of GDP)	2.5	2.5	2.5	1.8	1.2	—

Source: Czechoslovak authorities.

[1]Includes subsidies paid by federal, republic, and local budgets. Data are according to state final account and hence not directly comparable with data in Table A2.

[2]In 1991, retail subsidies on coal and gas are included in subsidies for residential heating.

[3]Transfers to support restructuring, especially of the armaments industry.

Table A4. Developments in Wholesale and Consumer Prices
(January 1, 1977 = 100)[1]

		1986	1987	1988	1989	1990	1991 I	1991 II	1991 III
Wholesale prices									
Industry		126.9	127.0	127.0	126.1	131.7	205.0	224.6	223.9
Construction		123.6	123.6	123.6	120.9	128.6	171.2	193.0	199.2
Construction materials		137.1	137.1	137.1	135.6	138.2	212.0	229.0	230.5
	Weights[2]								
Consumer prices									
Goods and services	100.00	121.5	121.6	121.8	123.5	135.8	198.4	217.2	221.3
Foodstuffs	31.31	121.5	121.7	121.3	121.4	134.9	200.0	193.8	194.3
Industrial goods	43.27	118.8	119.0	119.4	122.4	135.5	204.8	243.6	245.4
Services	15.16	118.3	118.2	119.3	120.3	129.1	151.3	173.6	192.4
Of which:									
Rents and communal services	3.22[3]	114.7	114.7	114.7	114.7	114.9	118.2	148.7	269.8
Transport and communications	2.80	121.6	121.6	121.6	121.6	129.5	151.6	181.6	187.6
Public restaurants	10.26	135.9	135.9	136.7	138.1	149.8	232.7	232.4	234.0

Source: Czechoslovak authorities.
[1]From 1987, data have been compiled on a base of January 1, 1984 = 100, and, from 1991, on a base of January 1989 = 100. The data from these series have been combined in this table.
[2]As of January 1, 1984.
[3]Not including electricity and gas.

Table A5. Average Monthly Earnings in the State and Cooperative Sector
(Excluding agricultural cooperatives (JZDs))[1]

	1986	1987	1988	1989	1990	1991[2] Jan.–Sept.	1991[3]
				(In koruny)			
Total state and cooperative sector, excluding JZDs	2,927	2,985	3,054	3,123	3,239	3,526	3,710
Material sphere	3,009	3,066	3,138	3,211	3,325	3,625	3,810
Of which:							
Agriculture	2,986	3,048	3,145	3,258	3,403	3,442	3,460
Industry	3,086	3,139	3,204	3,277	3,370	3,727	4,000
Building and construction	3,258	3,332	3,395	3,478	3,569	3,730	3,960
Nonmaterial sphere	2,702	2,765	2,830	2,893	3,023	3,238	3,430
Of which:							
Education	2,704	2,768	2,835	2,876	2,957	3,065	3,270
Health	2,744	2,793	2,832	2,885	3,089	3,463	3,650

Source: Czechoslovak authorities.
[1]Includes wages, bonuses, and other payments.
[2]Excludes enterprises with fewer than one hundred employees.
[3]Estimated.

Table A6. Industrial Production[1]

	1986	1987	1988	1989	1990	1991 Jan.–Sept.
	(Annual percent change, at constant 1989 prices)					
Fuel (coal and gas)	–0.6	0.3	0.2	–3.2	–6.7	–2.0
Power	4.9	2.5	1.6	2.0	–2.2	–3.0
Iron metallurgy	1.5	1.9	0.9	0.3	–0.9	–15.7
Nonferrous metals	2.4	1.8	2.1	1.2	–5.5	–37.0
Chemicals and rubber	4.0	3.2	2.0	0.7	–8.7	–22.6
Machinery	4.4	3.3	2.3	0.4	–3.2	–24.4
Electrotechnical	9.2	9.3	7.1	3.9	–6.3	–34.9
Construction parts	2.0	2.2	3.8	0.3	–6.1	–28.7
Wood processing	2.9	2.6	2.4	0.5	–2.0	–18.6
Paper and cellulose	3.9	1.9	3.1	2.9	0.8	–13.0
Glass, ceramics, and porcelain	1.8	1.6	6.1	6.3	1.2	–22.6
Textiles	2.4	1.6	2.3	1.2	0.4	–31.2
Clothing	2.0	1.6	2.3	2.8	–4.8	–36.8
Leather processing	1.4	–0.5	1.7	0.3	–1.5	–31.4
Print	3.2	2.1	4.0	1.4	7.9	–22.5
Food and beverages	1.7	0.5	0.4	2.3	–2.0	–16.4
Frozen foods, spring water, and tobacco products	3.6	4.5	2.4	4.7	1.7	–19.7
Other	2.4	2.6	2.3	3.0	–3.7	–21.3
Total gross output	3.2	2.5	2.1	0.8	–3.5	–21.3

Source: Czechoslovak authorities.
[1]Production of goods—constant 1989 prices.

Table A7. Employment by Sector
(In thousands, yearly average)

	1986	1987	1988	1989	1990[1]	1991[2]
Total employment[3]	7,775	7,824	7,875	7,901	7,873	7,350
Material sphere	5,846	5,874	5,882	5,868	5,787	5,250
Agriculture	861	853	839	811	795	. . .
Industry	2,923	2,941	2,951	2,954	2,870	. . .
Construction	685	695	700	701	731	. . .
Other	1,377	1,385	1,392	1,402	1,391	. . .
Nonmaterial sphere	1,929	1,950	1,993	2,033	2,086	2,100
Education	455	461	472	480	473	. . .
Health	330	334	342	350	357	. . .
Transport (passenger)	156	156	157	159	167	. . .
Science, research, and development	177	179	181	182	163	. . .
Other	811	820	841	862	926	. . .
Memorandum items:						
Women in work force (percent)	45.9	46.0	45.9	45.7	44.3	. . .
Workers in the state and cooperative sector (percent)[4]	90.4	90.4	90.2	89.9	87.2	. . .
Average number of hours worked per week[5]	43.1	43.1	43.0	40.6	40.6	. . .

Source: Czechoslovak authorities (new series).
[1]Provisional data.
[2]Estimated data.
[3]Excluding trainees and women on maternity leave.
[4]Excluding agricultural cooperatives (JZDs).
[5]Manufacturing only, beginning 1989, excluding meal breaks.

Table A8. Balance of Payments in Convertible Currencies
(In millions of U.S. dollars)

	1986	1987	1988	1989	1990	1991[1] Jan.–Sept.
Current account	468	–59	–59	439	–1,104	–205
Trade balance	224	–124	–83	419	–785	–384
Exports, f.o.b.	4,293	4,544	5,014	5,442	5,994	5,732
Imports, f.o.b.	4,069	4,669	5,096	5,022	6,780	6,116
Services balance	281	113	74	55	–279	156
Receipts	1,724	1,764	1,809	1,842	2,146	1,770
Transportation	881	863	885	885	959	619
Travel	103	132	149	158	339	361
Income	271	311	336	390	442	92
Other	469	459	438	408	405	696
Expenditures	1,442	1,652	1,754	1,787	2,426	1,614
Transportation	532	571	585	592	700	296
Travel	70	80	114	179	410	260
Income	436	484	562	553	758	311
Other	405	517	474	462	558	746
Unrequited transfers (net)	–37	–47	–51	–35	–40	23
Private	–5	–5	–9	–5	–6	37
Official	–31	–42	–42	–30	–34	–13
Capital account	–12	390	367	326	326	917
Direct investment (net)[2]	—	—	—	256	181	503
Other long-term capital (net)	–378	303	7	–53	718	1,098
Credits received by Czechoslovakia	–111	379	360	120	758	810
Credits extended by Czechoslovakia	–268	–76	–352	–173	–40	288
Short-term capital (net)	366	86	360	123	–573	–684
Valuation changes	–108	–155	–209	19	–324[3]	341[3]
Errors and omissions	–89	84	108	–216	—	—
Overall balance	260	260	207	569	–1,102	1,053
Change in reserves (increase –)	–260	–260	–207	–569	1,102	–1,053

Source: Czechoslovak authorities.
[1]Preliminary data.
[2]For 1989–90, the amounts represent investment lending; only $10 million was in equity investment.
[3]From 1990 onward, valuation changes are given so as to include errors and omissions.

Table A9. Balance of Payments in Nonconvertible Currencies
(In millions of U.S. dollars)[1]

	1986	1987	1988	1989	1990	1991[2] Jan.-Sept.
Current account	–300	430	1,152	500	–206	746
Trade balance	–610	–146	468	–274	–714	566
Exports, f.o.b	9,202	10,645	10,017	8,769	5,744	1,759
Imports, f.o.b	9,812	10,791	9,549	9,043	6,457	1,193
Services balance	262	461	568	631	261	166
Receipts	1,258	1,457	1,444	1,521	1,076	324
Transportation	782	850	782	742	648	50
Travel	280	360	458	423	155	14
Income	57	61	74	112	85	72
Other	139	185	179	245	188	188
Expenditures	996	996	925	890	815	158
Transportation	435	439	403	386	335	7
Travel	279	330	286	251	242	10
Income	26	35	26	37	29	1
Other	256	192	210	217	209	140
Unrequited transfers (net)	48	115	116	143	247	14
Private	58	100	103	135	266	12
Official	–9	15	13	8	–19	2
Capital account	84	–498	–1,260	–615	228	648
Direct investment (net)	. . .	. . .	. . .	–0	18	3
Other long-term capital (net)	–13	–88	–288	–713	–241	–176
Credits received by Czechoslovakia	–19	–4	8	–0	–2	–18
Credits extended by Czechoslovakia	6	–84	–296	–712	–240	–158
Short-term capital (net)	97	–410	–972	99	451	–474
Valuation changes	–7	62	34	–22	–22[3]	–98[3]
Errors and omissions	222	5	74	137	. . .	. . .
Overall balance	—	—	—	—	—	—

Source: Czechoslovak authorities.
[1]For 1986–90, data vis-à-vis the CMEA in transferable rubles were converted into U.S. dollars using cross rates.
[2]Preliminary data.
[3]From 1990 onward, valuation changes are given so as to include errors and omissions.

Table A10. Geographical Composition of Exports and Imports[1]
(In percent)

	1986	1987	1988	1989	1990	1991 QI–QIII
Exports, f.o.b.	100.0	100.0	100.0	100.0	100.0	100.0
Socialist countries	65.9	68.0	64.5	60.8	49.0	39.4
Of which: China	1.6	1.9	2.8	2.6	1.9	0.9
Yugoslavia	4.0	3.7	3.1	3.3	3.5	5.6
CMEA	60.3	62.3	58.5	54.9	43.4	32.4
Of which: Bulgaria	2.7	2.9	2.7	2.3	1.4	0.1
Former GDR	7.3	7.5	6.8	6.6	4.3	. . .
Hungary	4.2	4.6	4.3	4.0	4.1	4.4
Poland	7.1	7.9	8.1	8.5	6.2	6.7
Former U.S.S.R.	35.7	35.9	33.6	30.5	25.2	19.8
Nonsocialist countries	34.1	32.0	35.5	39.2	51.0	60.6
Industrial countries	23.1	23.1	26.5	31.1	42.4	51.4
Of which: Austria	3.5	3.3	0.0	4.6	5.9	5.7
France	1.3	1.3	1.5	1.8	2.6	2.5
Italy	1.5	1.5	1.7	2.1	3.1	4.1
Germany	6.8	6.7	7.5	8.3	12.8	24.6[2]
United Kingdom	1.5	1.8	2.0	2.0	2.6	2.0
Netherlands	1.2	1.1	1.3	1.5	2.2	3.0
Sweden	. . .	. . .	. . .	0.8	0.9	0.9
United States	0.5	0.5	0.6	0.6	0.8	0.9
Developing countries	9.8	7.6	7.6	8.0	8.6	9.2
Of which: India	0.6	0.6	0.7	0.8	0.9	0.5
Saudi Arabia	. . .	. . .	. . .	0.1	0.3	1.5
Syria	1.1	0.3	0.3	0.6	0.2	0.9
Brazil	0.3	0.1	0.2	0.2	0.2	0.2
Imports, f.o.b.	100.0	100.0	100.0	100.0	100.0	100.0
Socialist countries	68.4	67.6	63.2	62.3	51.2	44.1
Of which: China	2.4	1.7	2.5	2.8	3.4	1.3
Yugoslavia	3.0	3.2	3.1	3.3	3.3	2.3
CMEA	62.9	62.6	57.4	56.1	44.4	40.1
Of which: Bulgaria	2.7	4.3	2.5	2.2	1.2	0.6
Former GDR	8.0	8.5	8.2	7.8	8.2	. . .
Hungary	4.6	4.6	4.2	4.9	3.4	2.0
Poland	7.3	8.2	8.3	8.6	8.6	5.0
Former U.S.S.R.	37.6	36.2	31.3	29.6	21.6	31.7
Nonsocialist countries	31.6	32.4	36.8	37.7	48.8	55.9
Industrial countries	24.7	26.3	30.1	31.1	42.6	46.2
Of which: Austria	4.1	4.5	5.2	5.5	9.7	7.2
France	1.3	1.4	1.6	1.6	1.8	2.3
Italy	1.6	1.8	1.8	1.7	2.3	3.3
Germany	7.3	8.2	9.1	9.3	13.3	19.2[2]
United Kingdom	1.8	1.7	2.1	2.2	2.9	1.8
Netherlands	1.0	1.0	1.2	1.0	1.3	1.8
United States	0.4	0.2	0.4	0.4	0.6	1.9
Developing countries	5.7	5.1	5.4	6.6	6.2	9.7
Of which: India	0.5	0.6	0.8	1.5	1.1	0.3
Iran	. . .	. . .	. . .	0.5	0.8	2.7
Syria	0.1	0.3	0.2	0.2	0.1	0.1
Brazil	0.3	0.4	0.5	0.8	0.8	1.2

Source: Czechoslovak authorities.
[1]The terms "socialist" and "nonsocialist" here follow previously defined groupings. Socialist countries comprise former CMEA members, China, North Korea, and Yugoslavia.
[2]Includes former GDR.

Table A11. Commodity Composition of Exports, Standard International Trade Classification (SITC)[1]
(In millions of U.S. dollars)

SITC Category	Description	1986	1987	1988	1989	1990	1991[2]
0	Food and live animals	409	437	496	670	655	740
1	Beverages and tobacco	51	57	56	52	50	90
2	Inedible crude materials, except fuels	482	515	426	532	448	510
3	Minerals, fuels, lubricants, and related materials	581	661	616	751	522	400
33	Petroleum and petroleum products	(226)	(314)	(269)	(261)	(11)	(95)
4	Animal and vegetable oils and fats	9	3	15	20	41	20
5	Chemicals	888	1,064	1,229	1,092	1,082	1,130
6	Manufactured goods, classified chiefly by material	2,553	2,839	2,809	3,243	3,073	3,010
7	Machinery and transport equipment	6,757	7,644	7,035	6,416	4,696	2,970
8	Miscellaneous manufactured articles	1,500	1,697	1,590	1,397	1,248	1,330
9	Miscellaneous transactions and commodities not classified according to kind	198	173	624	283	175	—
	Total SITC 0–9	13,425	15,092	14,894	14,454	11,992	10,200
	Memorandum item:						
	Exchange rate (Kcs per U.S. dollar)	15.00	13.68	14.36	15.05	17.95	29.60

Source: Czechoslovak authorities.
[1]Data were converted from koruny at average commercial exchange rate for each period.
[2]Estimated.

Table A12. Commodity Composition of Imports, Standard International Trade Classification (SITC)[1]

(In millions of U.S. dollars)

SITC Category	Description	1986	1987	1988	1989	1990	1991[2]
0	Food and live animals	952	933	1,034	990	747	510
1	Beverages and tobacco	120	129	115	101	107	110
2	Inedible crude materials, except fuels	1,153	1,249	1,226	1,250	1,103	1,010
3	Minerals, fuels, lubricants, and related materials	3,476	3,562	2,778	2,336	1,901	2,940
33	Petroleum and petroleum products	(2,293)	(2,314)	(1,729)	(1,410)	(1,177)	(1,640)
4	Animal and vegetable oils and fats	50	40	55	52	74	35
5	Chemicals	1,102	1,234	1,269	1,333	1,353	1,010
6	Manufactured goods, classified chiefly by material	1,429	1,453	1,354	1,486	1,414	990
7	Machinery and transport equipment	4,330	5,368	5,281	5,271	4,950	2,800
8	Miscellaneous manufactured articles	728	840	901	878	1,209	680
9	Miscellaneous transactions and commodities not classified according to kind	345	434	582	435	415	15
	Total SITC 0–9	13,683	15,241	14,593	14,266	13,271	10,100
	Memorandum item:						
	Exchange rate (Kcs per U.S. dollar)	15.00	13.68	14.36	15.05	17.95	29.60

Source: Czechoslovak authorities.
[1] Data were converted from koruny at average commercial exchange rate for each period.
[2] Estimated.

Table A13. External Debt in Convertible and Nonconvertible Currencies

(In millions of U.S. dollars; end of period)

	1986	1987	1988	1989	1990	1991 Jan.–Sept.
Debt in convertible currencies	5,567	6,657	7,281	7,915	8,075	8,766
Medium- and long-term	2,877	3,581	3,874	4,328	5,172	6,061
By maturity:						
One to five years[1]	1,540	2,059	2,147	1,952	1,915	3,786
Over five years	1,337	1,522	1,728	2,377	3,257	2,275
By creditor:						
Foreign banks	2,042	2,154	2,228	2,628	3,290	3,273
Of which: trade related	. . .	. . .	. . .	. . .	. . .	. . .
Governments	—	—	—	—	—	—
Multilateral institutions	—	—	—	—	—	1,338
Suppliers	781	1,164	1,375	1,432	1,583	1,202
Former CMEA countries and institutions	54	262	272	268	258	248
By debtor:						
Banking system	2,095	2,417	2,499	2,574	3,040	3,920
Government	—	—	—	—	—	225
Corporations	781	1,164	1,375	1,754	2,132	1,916
Short-term	2,691	3,076	3,406	3,587	2,903	2,705
Debt in nonconvertible currencies	1,147	1,000	525	776	1,129	1,518
Medium- and long-term	68	71	70	70	53	29
Of which:						
One to five years	32	41	40	29	53	29
Over five years	36	30	30	41	—	—
Short-term	1,079	929	454	706	1,076	1,490
Total external debt	6,715	7,657	7,805	8,691	9,214	10,284
Of which:						
Medium- and long-term	2,945	3,652	3,945	4,398	5,235	6,090
Short-term	3,770	4,005	3,861	4,293	3,979	4,194
Memorandum items:						
Total external debt, convertible currrencies (percent of exports of goods and nonfactor services in convertible currencies)	97	111	112	115	105	87
Stock of joint venture equity owned by foreigners (million U.S. dollars)	—	—	—	—	10	513

Source: Czechoslovak authorities.
[1]Estimated.

Table A14. Exchange Rates

	1987	1988	1989	1990 QI	1990 QII	1990 QIII	1990 QIV	1991 QI	1991 QII	1991 QIII
				(In koruny per U.S. dollar)						
Average during period										
Official rate[1]	5.47	5.32	. . .	. . .	. . .	. . .	. . .	. . .	. . .	. . .
Commercial rate[2,3]	13.68	14.36	15.05	16.53	16.62	15.99	22.67	27.88	30.32	30.53
Noncommercial rate[2,3]	9.57	9.31	9.75	. . .	. . .	. . .	. . .	. . .	. . .	. . .
Auction rate[4]	. . .	. . .	121.24	78.77	47.99	34.31	41.15	. . .	. . .	. . .
Parallel market rate[5]	27.78	33.44	42.39	41.51	36.26	33.32	41.02	34.08	31.69	32.51
Tourist rate[6]	. . .	. . .	. . .	37.55	30.15	26.97	30.99	. . .	. . .	. . .
				(In koruny per transferable ruble)						
Official rate[1]	8.00	8.00	. . .	. . .	. . .	. . .	. . .	. . .	. . .	. . .
Commercial rate[7,8]	11.20	10.40	10.00	9.00	9.00	9.00	9.00	. . .	. . .	. . .
Noncommercial rate[8,9]	16.00	16.00	15.00	12.00	12.00	12.00	12.00	. . .	. . .	. . .
				(In koruny per U.S. dollar)						
End of period										
Official rate[1]	5.20	5.30	. . .	. . .	. . .	. . .	. . .	. . .	. . .	. . .
Commercial rate[2,3]	13.00	14.31	14.29	16.81	16.51	15.71	28.00	30.15	31.03	29.85
Noncommercial rate[2,3]	9.10	9.28	9.26	. . .	. . .	. . .	. . .	. . .	. . .	. . .
Auction rate[4]	. . .	. . .	114.35	59.15	39.36	31.04	39.40	. . .	. . .	. . .
Parallel market rate[5]	30.54	40.35	43.48	41.49	35.57	33.56	45.65	36.24	32.90	30.65
Tourist rate[6]	. . .	. . .	. . .	36.96	27.85	26.49	28.00	. . .	. . .	. . .
				(In koruny per transferable ruble)						
Official rate[1]	8.00	8.00	. . .	. . .	. . .	. . .	. . .	. . .	. . .	. . .
Commercial rate[7,8]	11.20	10.40	10.00	9.00	9.00	9.00	9.00	. . .	. . .	. . .
Noncommercial rate[8,9]	16.00	16.00	15.00	12.00	12.00	12.00	12.00	. . .	. . .	. . .

Sources: Czechoslovak authorities; and Schweizerischer Bankverein.

[1]Official rate was abolished from January 1, 1989.

[2]Until December 31, 1988, the commercial rate equaled the official rate multiplied by certain coefficients.

[3]The commercial and noncommercial rates were unified from January 8, 1990.

[4]First auction took place on August 30, 1989; last auction took place on December 12, 1990.

[5]Data from Schweizerischer Bankverein.

[6]Separate tourist rates were in effect during 1990, then unified with the commercial rate on December 28, 1990.

[7]This rate applied to trade with the former GDR, Romania, and the former U.S.S.R. The rates for Bulgaria and Poland were 5 percent lower, and that for Hungary 10 percent higher than the rates shown.

[8]Trade with the former CMEA countries was denominated in convertible currencies from January 1, 1991.

[9]This rate was used for interstate settlements and differed according to individual countries. The data in the table represent those for the former U.S.S.R.

References

Aghevli, Bijan, Mohsin Khan, and Peter Montiel, *Exchange Rate Policy in Developing Countries: Some Analytical Issues*, IMF Occasional Paper No. 78 (Washington: International Monetary Fund, 1991).

Blanchard, Olivier, and others, *Reform in Eastern Europe* (Cambridge, Massachusetts: MIT Press, 1991).

Borensztein, Eduardo, "Comments on David Lipton and Jeffrey Sachs, 'Privatization in Eastern Europe: The Case of Poland,' Roman Frydman and Andrzej Rapaczynski, 'Markets and Institutions in Large-Scale Privatization,' and Manuel Hinds, 'A Note on the Privatization of Socialized Enterprises in Poland'" in *Reforming Central and Eastern European Economies*, ed. by V. Corbo, F. Coricelli, and J. Bossak (Washington: World Bank, 1991).

Calvo, Guillermo, and Fabrizio Coricelli, "Stabilizing a Previously Centrally Planned Economy: Poland 1990," *Economic Policy* (forthcoming, 1992).

Calvo, Guillermo, and Jacob Frenkel (1991a), "From Centrally Planned to Market Economy: The Road from CPE to PCPE," *Staff Papers*, International Monetary Fund, Vol. 38 (June 1991), pp. 268–99.

———(1991b), "Obstacles to Transforming Centrally-Planned Economies: The Role of Capital Markets," NBER Working Paper No. 3116 (Cambridge, Massachusetts: National Bureau of Economic Research, July 1991).

Collins, Susan, and Dani Rodrik, *Eastern Europe and the Soviet Union in the World Economy* (Washington: Institute for International Economics, 1991).

Corbo, Vittorio, Fabrizio Coricelli, and Jan Bossak (eds.), *Reforming Central and Eastern European Economies: Initial Results and Challenges* (Washington: World Bank, 1991).

Demekas, Dimitri, and Mohsin Khan, *The Romanian Economic Reform Program*, IMF Occasional Paper No. 89 (Washington: International Monetary Fund, 1991).

Diwan, Ishac, and Fernando Saldanha, "Long Term Prospects in Eastern Europe: The Role of External Finance in an Era of Change," (Washington: World Bank, 1991).

Dornbusch, Rudiger, "Priorities of Economic Reform in Eastern Europe and the Soviet Union," CEPR Occasional Paper No. 5 (London: Center for Economic Policy Research, 1991).

———, and Holger Wolf, "Monetary Overhang and Reforms in the 1940s," NBER Working Paper No. 3456 (Cambridge, Massachusetts: National Bureau of Economic Research, 1990).

Dyba, Karel, and Jan Svejnar, "Czechoslovakia: Recent Economic Developments and Prospects," *American Economic Review*, Vol. 81 (May 1991), pp. 185–90.

Fischer, Stanley, and Alan Gelb, "Issues in the Reform of Socialist Economies," in *Reforming Central and Eastern European Economies*, ed. by V. Corbo, F. Coricelli, and J. Bossak (Washington: World Bank, 1991).

Government of the Czech and Slovak Federal Republic, "Scénář Ekonomicke Reformy" (unpublished; Prague, August 30, 1990).

Hinds, Manuel, "A Note on the Privatization of Socialized Enterprises in Poland," in *Reforming Central and Eastern European Economies*, ed. by V. Corbo, F. Coricelli, and J. Bossak (Washington: World Bank, 1991).

Hrnčíř, Miroslav, and Jan Klacek, "Stabilization Policies and Currency Convertibility in Czechoslovakia," *European Economy: The Path of Reform in Central and Eastern Europe*, Commission of the European Communities, Directorate-General for Economic and Financial Affairs (Brussels), Special edition No. 2 (1991), pp. 17–39.

Klaus, Vaclav, "Policy Dilemmas of Eastern European Reforms: Notes of an Insider," *Economic Review*, Federal Reserve Bank of Kansas City, Vol. 75 (September/October 1990), pp. 5–8.

Kornai, Janos, "Soft Budget Constraint," *Kyklos*, Vol. 39 (1986), pp. 3–30.

Lipton, David, and Jeffrey Sachs, "Privatization in Eastern Europe: The Case of Poland," *Brookings Papers on Economic Activity: 2* (Washington: The Brookings Institution, 1990), pp. 293–341.

Portes, Richard, "Transition to Convertibility for Eastern Europe and the USSR," CEPR Discussion Paper No. 500 (London: Center for Economic Policy Research, January 1991).

Prust, Jim, and IMF Staff Team, *The Czech and Slovak Federal Republic: An Economy in Transition*, IMF Occasional Paper No. 72 (Washington: International Monetary Fund, 1990).

Solimano, Andres, "The Economies of Central and Eastern Europe: An Historical and International Perspective," in *Reforming Central and Eastern European Economies*, ed. by V. Corbo, F. Coricelli, and J. Bossak (Washington: World Bank, 1991).

Tanzi, Vito, "Mobilization of Savings in Eastern European Countries: The Role of the State," IMF Working Paper 91/4 (Washington: International Monetary Fund, January 1991).

Recent Occasional Papers of the International Monetary Fund

92. Stabilization and Structural Reform in the Czech and Slovak Federal Republic: First Stage, by Bijan B. Aghevli, Eduardo Borensztein, and Tessa van der Willigen. 1992.

91. Economic Policies for a New South Africa, edited by Desmond Lachman and Kenneth Bercuson with a staff team comprising Daudi Ballali, Robert Corker, Charalambos Christofides, and James Wein. 1992.

90. The Internationalization of Currencies: An Appraisal of the Japanese Yen, by George S. Tavlas and Yuzuru Ozeki. 1992.

89. The Romanian Economic Reform Program, by Dimitri G. Demekas and Mohsin S. Khan. 1991.

88. Value-Added Tax: Administrative and Policy Issues, edited by Alan A. Tait. 1991.

87. Financial Assistance from Arab Countries and Arab Regional Institutions, by Pierre van den Boogaerde. 1991.

86. Ghana: Adjustment and Growth, 1983–91, by Ishan Kapur, Michael T. Hadjimichael, Paul Hilbers, Jerald Schiff, and Philippe Szymczak. 1991.

85. Thailand: Adjusting to Success—Current Policy Issues, by David Robinson, Yangho Byeon, and Ranjit Teja with Wanda Tseng. 1991.

84. Financial Liberalization, Money Demand, and Monetary Policy in Asian Countries, by Wanda Tseng and Robert Corker. 1991.

83. Economic Reform in Hungary Since 1968, by Anthony R. Boote and Janos Somogyi. 1991.

82. Characteristics of a Successful Exchange Rate System, by Jacob A. Frenkel, Morris Goldstein, and Paul R. Masson. 1991.

81. Currency Convertibility and the Transformation of Centrally Planned Economies, by Joshua E. Greene and Peter Isard. 1991.

80. Domestic Public Debt of Externally Indebted Countries, by Pablo E. Guidotti and Manmohan S. Kumar. 1991.

79. The Mongolian People's Republic: Toward a Market Economy, by Elizabeth Milne, John Leimone, Franek Rozwadowski, and Padej Sukachevin. 1991.

78. Exchange Rate Policy in Developing Countries: Some Analytical Issues, by Bijan B. Aghevli, Mohsin S. Khan, and Peter J. Montiel. 1991.

77. Determinants and Systemic Consequences of International Capital Flows, by Morris Goldstein, Donald J. Mathieson, David Folkerts-Landau, Timothy Lane, J. Saúl Lizondo, and Liliana Rojas-Suárez. 1991.

76. China: Economic Reform and Macroeconomic Management, by Mario Blejer, David Burton, Steven Dunaway, and Gyorgy Szapary. 1991.

75. German Unification: Economic Issues, edited by Leslie Lipschitz and Donogh McDonald. 1990.

74. The Impact of the European Community's Internal Market on the EFTA, by Richard K. Abrams, Peter K. Cornelius, Per L. Hedfors, and Gunnar Tersman. 1990.

73. The European Monetary System: Developments and Perspectives, by Horst Ungerer, Jouko J. Hauvonen, Augusto Lopez-Claros, and Thomas Mayer. 1990.

72. The Czech and Slovak Federal Republic: An Economy in Transition, by Jim Prust and an IMF Staff Team. 1990.

71. MULTIMOD Mark II: A Revised and Extended Model, by Paul Masson, Steven Symansky, and Guy Meredith. 1990.

70. The Conduct of Monetary Policy in the Major Industrial Countries: Instruments and Operating Procedures, by Dallas S. Batten, Michael P. Blackwell, In-Su Kim, Simon E. Nocera, and Yuzuru Ozeki. 1990.

69. International Comparisons of Government Expenditure Revisited: The Developing Countries, 1975–86, by Peter S. Heller and Jack Diamond. 1990.

68. Debt Reduction and Economic Activity, by Michael P. Dooley, David Folkerts-Landau, Richard D. Haas, Steven A. Symansky, and Ralph W. Tryon. 1990.

67. The Role of National Saving in the World Economy: Recent Trends and Prospects, by Bijan B. Aghevli, James M. Boughton, Peter J. Montiel, Delano Villanueva, and Geoffrey Woglom. 1990.

66. The European Monetary System in the Context of the Integration of European Financial Markets, by David Folkerts-Landau and Donald J. Mathieson. 1989.

65. Managing Financial Risks in Indebted Developing Countries, by Donald J. Mathieson, David Folkerts-Landau, Timothy Lane, and Iqbal Zaidi. 1989.

64. The Federal Republic of Germany: Adjustment in a Surplus Country, by Leslie Lipschitz, Jeroen Kremers, Thomas Mayer, and Donogh McDonald. 1989.

63. Issues and Developments in International Trade Policy, by Margaret Kelly, Naheed Kirmani, Miranda Xafa, Clemens Boonekamp, and Peter Winglee. 1988.

62. The Common Agricultural Policy of the European Community: Principles and Consequences, by Julius Rosenblatt, Thomas Mayer, Kasper Bartholdy, Dimitrios Demekas, Sanjeev Gupta, and Leslie Lipschitz. 1988.

61. Policy Coordination in the European Monetary System. Part I: The European Monetary System: A Balance Between Rules and Discretion, by Manuel Guitián. Part II: Monetary Coordination Within the European Monetary System: Is There a Rule? by Massimo Russo and Giuseppe Tullio. 1988.

60. Policies for Developing Forward Foreign Exchange Markets, by Peter J. Quirk, Graham Hacche, Viktor Schoofs, and Lothar Weniger. 1988.

59. Measurement of Fiscal Impact: Methodological Issues, edited by Mario I. Blejer and Ke-Young Chu. 1988.

58. The Implications of Fund-Supported Adjustment Programs for Poverty: Experiences in Selected Countries, by Peter S. Heller, A. Lans Bovenberg, Thanos Catsambas, Ke-Young Chu, and Parthasarathi Shome. 1988.

57. The Search for Efficiency in the Adjustment Process: Spain in the 1980s, by Augusto Lopez-Claros. 1988.

56. Privatization and Public Enterprises, by Richard Hemming and Ali M. Mansoor. 1988.

55. Theoretical Aspects of the Design of Fund-Supported Adjustment Programs: A Study by the Research Department of the International Monetary Fund. 1987.

54. Protection and Liberalization: A Review of Analytical Issues, by W. Max Corden. 1987.

53. Floating Exchange Rates in Developing Countries: Experience with Auction and Interbank Markets, by Peter J. Quirk, Benedicte Vibe Christensen, Kyung-Mo Huh, and Toshihiko Sasaki. 1987.

52. Structural Reform, Stabilization, and Growth in Turkey, by George Kopits. 1987.

51. The Role of the SDR in the International Monetary System: Studies by the Research and Treasurer's Departments of the International Monetary Fund. 1987.

50. Strengthening the International Monetary System: Exchange Rates, Surveillance, and Objective Indicators, by Andrew Crockett and Morris Goldstein. 1987.

49. Islamic Banking, by Zubair Iqbal and Abbas Mirakhor. 1987.

Note: For information on the title and availability of Occasional Papers not listed, please consult the IMF *Publications Catalog* or contact IMF Publication Services. Occasional Paper Nos. 5–26 are $5.00 a copy (academic rate: $3.00); Nos. 27–64 are $7.50 a copy (academic rate: $4.50); Nos. 65–86 are $10.00 a copy (academic rate: $7.50); and from No. 87 on, the price is $15.00 a copy (academic rate: $12.00).